His Angels

JOY HANEY

Guideposts®

CARMEL • NEW YORK 10512

Contents

Acknowledgments   ix

Preface   xi

Introduction   xiii

CHAPTER 1
His Angels   1

CHAPTER 2
To Protect and Bear Us Up   13

    An Angel on Board   13

    The Blinded Terrorists   14

    The Man with the Lunchbox   14

    The Angel Who Put My Car in Reverse   15

    The Underwater Angel   16

    Guards on the Rooftop 17

    The Guardian Angel   17

    The Bronze Cape   18

    An Angel Swimming Underwater   20

    Angels in the Fire   21

    Ask for Woody   23

CHAPTER 3

To Bring Messages of Hope and Healing 27

The Ethiopian Angel   27

Marcus's Miracle   30

The Emergency Room Angels   31

The Healing Angel   33

The Glowing Angel   34

The Doctor Who Kept Watch   35

The Angel Came on Wednesday   36

CHAPTER 4

To Send God's Provision 41

A Special Delivery   41

Two Angels and a Truck out of Nowhere   42

The Folded Sheets   44

The Lady in White   46

The Mysterious Messenger   47

The Invisible Messenger   49

The White-Coated Angel   50

CHAPTER 5

To Work with Us in God's Kingdom 55

Angels in Church   55

The Flying Angel   56

The White Form   57

Shoulder-to-Shoulder Angels   58

The Tall, Shiny Angel   58

The Authoritative Angel   59

The Warring Angel   60

The Gentle Angel   60

CHAPTER 6

To Help Us with the Difficulties of Everyday Life   65

Angel in the Courtroom   65

Heaven's Connection—the Free Phone Call   66

The Other Person's Footprints   67

The Invisible Hand   68

The Name on the Mailbox   69

The Lost Key   70

Angel in the Fog   70

The Light in the Blizzard   72

CHAPTER 7

To Help in the Time of Crisis   75

The Little Girl Angel   75

The Invisible Mercedes-Benz   76

The Uncanny SOS   77

The Invisible Companion   78

Pulled from the Flood   79

Contents

Out of the Mire   80

The Other Two Passengers   81

CHAPTER 8

To Soothe Our Fears in the Time of Sickness and Distress   85

The White Light   85

The Fourth Man   86

The Soft Hand   89

The Room Full of Angels   90

Nurse with a Smile   91

CHAPTER 9

To Help When We Pray Heartfelt Prayers   95

The Mysterious Magazine   95

The Fantastic Reunion   96

The Flying Van   97

Taught by an Angel   98

The Shackles Fell Off   99

The Eastern Airlines Employee   100

CHAPTER 10

To Encourage Us   105

Two Extra Place Settings   105

Twelve Angels   107

The Bright Light   109

Contents

The Immense Angel   110

The Rush of Peace   111

Stranger at the Spring   112

CHAPTER 11

Speak Messages from God   117

~ Acknowledgments ~

I WISH TO THANK the following people to whom I talked or whom I myself interviewed concerning their stories in this book: Rev. James Kilgore, Ima Jean Kilgore, Rev. Bennie DeMerchant, Theresa DeMerchant, Bruce Howell, Brenda Aguirre, Gail Rozell, Sherrie Woodward, Grace Ann Gee, Marilyn Turner, Kay LaCoss, Wanda Snyder, Priscilla McGruder, Nancy Hunt, James Spencer, Heather Monteforte, Pete Lopez, Dr. Pam Hanley, Rev. Harold Clemons, Rev. B. J. Wilmoth, Doris Rome, Yoshi Brown, Katherine Spacek, Kelly Mason, Rev. Norman Zeno, Rev. Randy Graham, Michelle Peters, Mildred Watts, Brenda Cox and Rev. Ed Snyder, Cindi Freidli, Angela Haney and Betty Whayne.

I also want to thank all the others who cared enough to share their stories with me. Even though I did not speak with them personally, their contributions have helped make this book possible.

Special thanks goes to Brent Regnart who has been my editorial assistant for several years. He is a man who wears several hats—and wears this one well.

I want to thank my daughter-in-law, Kim Haney, a terrific graphic artist, who has helped me with many of my projects.

∾

~ *Preface* ~

ANGELS ARE GOD'S SERVANTS. They do his bidding. That is why it is important to praise and worship God whenever we are helped by an angel or receive supernatural help; for it is God who sends angels and supernatural help in the time of need. That is why I have titled this book *His Angels*.

When John the Revelator was shown the glories of the heavens by an angel, he wanted to worship the angel, but he was stopped. The angel said, "'Do not do it! I am a fellow servant with you and with your brothers the prophets and of all who keep the words of this book. Worship God.'" (Revelation 22:8–9, NIV).

~ Introduction ~

FOR THE LAST EIGHTEEN YEARS, it seems as if God has illuminated my thoughts and given me inspiration to write. This book is my thirty-fourth. I have never had to chew on a pencil thinking, "What can I write next?" Each book has been like a heavenly assignment. Even though writing a book requires much work, thought and diligence to be able to finish it, the energy expended has not wearied me to the point of quitting, because I have felt as though I was on a mission.

In the winter of 1995, there came to me a strong impression to write a book on the subject of angels. In the spring of 96, I was speaking at a women's conference in Pennsylvania and briefly mentioned that I was working on a book about angels. When I asked if any of them had ever had an angel experience, over twenty-five women responded that they had. In my later travels, speaking in other parts of the United States, I discovered more and more people who had angel stories.

I have had to lay this book aside several times because of all the other activities in which I am involved. Also, during this time, inspiration for several other books came to me and seemed to signal for my attention. But during the past few months my mind has been drawn back to this book, *His Angels*. It has been a pure delight and renewal of faith to research and gather stories about the activities of the angelic realm. The marvelous stories in this book all happened to normal people. The incredible events altered the course of their lives and made them more aware of God's great love for them and the workings of His vast kingdom.

In my own experiences with angels, the year 1988 was a turning point. One night, I had a dream that was so vivid it woke me, and its memory has never diminished. I remember climbing out of bed and going into my home office about 4:00 in the morning, with tears running down my cheeks and the thought of Genesis 24 in my mind. I opened my Bible and there was the story of Abraham sending his servant to go in search of a wife for his son Issac. In giving his servant this vision, Abraham had him take an oath. That was what my dream was about.

In my dream I saw a beautiful white throne surrounded by dazzling light and a feeling of grandeur. Leading up to the throne was what looked like a strip of deep red carpet. On either side of the carpet angels were lined up, shoulder to shoulder. They were looking at me as I walked up the carpet towards the throne. Sitting on the throne was Jesus. All the angels were saying to me in strong tones, "An oath, an oath, you've got to take an oath!"

The passion and energy of the dream left me shaken, but I felt so special to be called into God's service. Kneeling in my home office in tears, I felt a strong presence enter the room, and I said the words, "I will take an oath. I will go and help people find you. I will be your servant and bring you a bride, as the servant took an oath to find Issac one." Since that time, there have been instances where people have shared with me that while I was speaking, they saw angels near me. Three of those stories are included in this book.

I am a mother of five beautiful children, three of whom are married. We have wonderful times together. My husband, Kenneth, and I have been married thirty-six years as of October 14th. We now have four grand-children. We have given our lives to helping people. For twenty-five years Kenneth has been pastor of Christian Life Center, which has grown to over four thousand people. Some of the members have shared their angel stories with me, and you will find them in these pages. This book is a collection of extraordinary stories that have happened to ordinary people. They are proof that there is a spirit world that is an integral part of our lives.

I feel, and have felt in the past, that the angels of God are very much a part of our lives. I remember hearing stories about the Six-Day War in 1969, when men who were pilots in the Israeli Army reported seeing men riding on the wings of the plane they were piloting. Several men who were interviewed concerning this war stated that angels helped them win. A war was won by a country that had all the odds stacked against them, and with divine intervention, it only took six days.

Our family has also witnessed many miracles: things that could not have happened without divine intervention. We have sensed the hidden hand of God moving silently but majestically in our lives. Although we have walked through deep sorrows and disappointments, and have faced many crises, God and His angels have been there with us.

I hope that when you have finished reading this book you will have a new understanding of a phenomenon that perhaps you have only dimly sensed. I hope it will cause you to look back over your own life and recall certain unexplainable happenings that left you puzzled and in wonderment. Then you will realize that you are not alone; that God is only a prayer away, and that He has His angels waiting to help you when you call upon Him. There is definitely an invisible world that is very busy working in your behalf.

∿

*"Millions of spiritual creatures walk the earth
Unseen, both when we wake, and when we sleep:
All these with ceaseless praise his works behold
Both day and night."*

—JOHN MILTON (1608–74)
Paradise Lost, Book IV, ll 677–80.

His Angels

Behold, I send an Angel before thee, to keep thee in the way.
—EXODUS 23:20

N AUGUST 1988, an article appeared in *Reader's Digest* entitled, "A Boy, a Snake and an Angel." Henry Hurt told the story of twelve-year-old Mark Durrance. He had gone out with his dog Bobo and his BB gun to do some shooting in the scrubland near their Florida home.

As Mark and Bobo were heading home, the boy spotted a bird in a cabbage palm. With his eyes fixed on the bird, he leaped over a ditch. He landed on something that seemed to roll under the pressure of his right foot. Instantly Mark felt an explosion of pain. At first it was a numbing crush like an ax being slammed down on his foot. Then a searing jolt of furious heat savaged his lower leg....

The massive head of an Eastern diamondback rattlesnake was plastered across his foot. Its heavily muscled maw opened across the top of Mark's shoe in a ferocious grip. The fangs had pierced the leather and become embedded just in front of the anklebone. Scorched with pain, the boy stared down at the snake as it seemed to gnaw slowly and deliberately on his foot.

Then Mark was aware of his dog's loud snarling and snapping at the snake. Bobo kept darting in and nipping—ten or fiteen times—but the snake wouldn't let go. Then Bobo pounced and tore into the snake's head, and blood flew.

At that instant, Mark felt the serpent release its grip. He jerked his leg away, and the snake slithered off into the bushes.

Mark was 150 yards from his house.... The pain was overpowering. He felt weak all over, and everything started to go fuzzy. Though Mark did not know it, the rattlesnake's fangs had injected a massive amount of venom directly into a vein. The poison was racing through his body, launching multiple attacks upon his respiratory system, his heart, his body's ability to clot blood. It would take a miracle for the boy to cover 150 yards over rough terrain and then mount the steps to his door.

Bobby Durrance [Mark's father] was pruning the bushes in his front yard, when his oldest son, Buddy, came screaming: "Daddy! Mark's been snake bit!"...Bobby raced for the house and found Mark on the living-room floor, unconscious, his mother, Debbie, beside him.... The only words Mark uttered had come calmly and peacefully from his lips as he walked through the door: "I've been rattlesnake bit." Then he fell to the floor unconscious, violent convulsions racking his body.

Debbie tore at Mark's shoes and uncovered an ugly, purple mound that looked to be grapefruit-size on his right foot. Without a telephone, Debbie and Bobby knew they had to drive for help. They twisted a tourniquet around Mark's leg. Then, with their son in their arms, they ran to their pickup truck and took off at top speed for the health clinic seventeen miles away.

"Mark was completely limp," says Debbie. "I had him cradled in my arms.

I kept his nose against my face, and his breathing was getting fainter and fainter. The only thing I could do was pray."...

A mile short of the clinic, the truck began to sputter...then the engine cut off completely.... Bobby jumped out and frantically waved his arms. Drivers swerved around him. Bobby ran back to the truck and took Mark from Debbie's arms. He carried him to the middle of the road and held the boy's limp, almost breathless body up in the air like a flag.

One car slammed on its brakes. The driver, a Haitian farm worker, spoke no English, but he understood. He urged Debbie and her unconscious son into his car and followed Debbie's hand-motion directions to the clinic.

When the clinic staff realized Mark needed more help than they could give, they transferred him by ambulance to the hospital in Naples ten miles away. There four doctors and many nurses worked around the clock to keep Mark's cardiovascular system from collapsing. Then his kidneys shut down and he started hemorrhaging internally. Although the doctors gave him antivenom injections, after eight hours he was still critical, he was in a coma with blood seeping from his ears, mouth and eyes. His body was swollen, including his eyes.

Debbie never left the hospital. She sat for hours, praying over her son and comforting him: "He may have been in a coma, but I believed he might hear my words to him and to God."

On the third day, Mark began to regain consciousness; on the fourth, he was removed from the respirator. During the first few moments, doctors listened intently as Mark spoke to his parents. Though his voice was scratchy, he told with striking clarity about how he had jumped the ditch and landed on the rattlesnake. Laughter mingled with tears when Mark said he hoped his father was not angry with him for being so careless. To the doctors, this clarity was a sign that Mark's brain had not been damaged.

Then the doctors and nurses left the bedside. Only the boy's parents remained. Debbie rubbed her son's swollen brow and gently held his bloated hand. It was during these moments, when Mark and his parents were alone in this loving cocoon of humble thanksgiving, that the boy told them of an extraordinary event that took place in the desolate field—an occurrence that harks to the Old Testament's stirring accounts of men and angels.

Mark explained with perfect composure about a white-robed figure who appeared just when he knew that he could not walk the distance to the house. The figure took him in his arms and carried him across the field and up the steps.

"I know it was God," Mark said. "He had a deep voice. I felt calm. He picked me up and carried me all the way. He told me that I was going to be sick but not to worry, that I would make it. Then he went up into the sky. The last thing I remember was opening the door to our house." . . .

What Mark says happened can never be proved, but such things never lend themselves to proof. Somehow, the boy made it 150 yards over rough terrain and up 13 steps and then opened the door to his house. . . . "From a medical standpoint, I don't know how he could have done it," [one of his doctors said]. But Mark knows with absolute certainty. . . .

Mark's parents are deeply thankful for the doctors and nurses. They also wonder about the kindly Haitian farm worker. "I don't know what would have happened without that man," says Debbie. "By the time I went to thank him, he was gone. We never knew his name."

Angels visit us unawares many times. They are often unseen; many times they are seen but unrecognized. They can appear in any shape or form. The following story that was told in *Reader's Digest* many years ago is related by Billy Graham.

Dr. S. W. Mitchell, a celebrated Philadelphia neurologist, had gone to bed after an exceptionally tiring day. Suddenly he was awakened by someone knocking on his door. Opening it he found a little girl, poorly dressed and deeply upset. She told him her mother was very sick and asked him if he would please come with her. It was a bitterly cold, snowy night, but though he was bone tired, Dr. Mitchell dressed and followed the girl.

As *Reader's Digest* reports the story, he found the mother desperately ill with pneumonia. After arranging for medical care, he complimented the sick woman on the intelligence and persistence of her little daughter. The woman looked at him strangely and then said, "My daughter died a month ago." She added, "Her shoes and coat are in the coat closet there."

Dr. Mitchell, amazed and perplexed, went to the closet and opened the door. There hung the very coat worn by the little girl who had brought him to help her mother. It was warm and dry and could not possibly have been out in the wintry night.[1]

In an imperfect world filled with sickness, disease, heartache, hurt, disaster, pain and evil, there is also a perfect God who is good. He gives power to his angels to help us. They are working constantly to help those who call upon God for help.

A woman suddenly found herself in a head-on collision course with a large truck. She had time only to shut her eyes and say, "Jesus!"

Amazed that she had not crashed, she opened her eyes and found herself parked beside the road, the truck a short distance behind her.

"What happened?" she asked the truck driver who had come to her window.

---

[1]Quoted in Billy Graham, *Angels* (New York: Doubleday, 1975), pp. 2–13.

"Lady, you won't believe this," the ashen-faced man replied, "but you flew!"

Extraordinary things like this happen often, but they do not make news because they are so unbelievable. Experiences such as these are mulled over, silently thought about and told among family members with hushed voices of awe and wonderment. They happen on the highways, in homes, on the oceans, in wars and in places all around the world.

In his book *Angels*, Billy Graham tells the following story which he heard on a visit to American troops during the Korean War.

A small group of American marines in the First Division…had been trapped up north. With the thermometer at twenty degrees below zero, they were close to freezing to death. And they had had nothing to eat for six days. Surrender to the Chinese seemed their only hope for survival. But one of the men, a Christian pointed out certain verses of Scripture, and taught his comrades to sing a song of praise to God. Following this, they heard a crashing noise, and turned to see a wild boar rushing toward them. As they tried to jump out of his way, he suddenly stopped in his tracks. One of the soldiers raised his rifle to shoot, but before he could fire, the boar inexplicably toppled over…dead.…That night they feasted on meat, and began to regain their strength.

The next morning just as the sun was rising they heard another noise. Their fear that a Chinese patrol had discovered them suddenly vanished as they found themselves face to face with a South Korean who could speak English. He said, "I will show you out." He led them through the forest and mountains to safety behind their own lines. When they looked up to thank him, they found he had disappeared.[*]

---

[*]Graham, *Angels*, pp. 169–70.

In his book, *Moments With Angels,* Robert Strand tells the story of two teenage sisters, Cheriee and Susan, who had been shopping in a suburban mall. When they were ready to go home, it was dark, and very late! From the mall exit they saw their car, the only one left in that section of the parking lot.

Nervous, they waited, hoping some other customers would come along so they could walk out together. They were aware of the current crime wave in area shopping malls and remembered Dad's warning: "Don't stay too late!"

"Let's get with it...now!" Susan shifted her packages, pushed open the door and walked as fast as she could with Cheriee following, both looking from side to side.

They just made it! Cheriee shoved the key into the door lock, got in, reached across to open Susan's door. Then...they both heard the sound of running feet behind them. They turned to look and panicked—racing toward their car were two ominous looking men!

One of the men shouted, "We got you, you're not going anywhere!"

Susan jumped in and both locked their doors just in time.

With shaking hands, Cheriee turned the ignition switch. Nothing! She tried again and again...nothing! Click! Silence! No power! The men were ready to smash a window.

Knowing there were scant seconds of safety left, the girls joined hands and prayed! "Dear God," Susan pleaded, "give us a miracle in the name of Jesus!"

Again Cheriee turned the key...the engine roared to life and they raced out of the lot!

The girls cried all the way home, screeched into the driveway and pulled the car into the garage. Bursting into the house, they spilled their story to their parents. They held them both as they comforted two frightened daughters.

"You're safe...thank God, that's the main thing. But don't do it again," their father said. Then he frowned, "It's strange. That car has never failed to start. I'll just check it out now."

In the garage he raised the hood. After one stunned glance, he realized *who* had brought his daughters home safely that night! There was no battery in the car!

Inexplicable! Human reasoning cannot comprehend how an automobile can run without a battery. But there is an unseen world that is moving, pulsating and pregnant with miracles, filled with God's power, which people involved in desperate situations that are beyond their ability to deal with can draw on by appealing to God for help.

Margaret Baucom of Shreveport, Louisiana, a private-duty nurse, had been caring for an elderly man for several nights in a row. Usually her shift ended about seven. One morning however, the man's wife awakened early and told Margaret to go on home and get some much-needed sleep. Margaret pulled away from the house in somewhat of a fog, so tired that she forgot to press her automatic door lock. She would avoid the high-speed interstate, she decided, and take a slower route home. "It went through a tough section of town, but I assumed no one would be up at four A.M.," she says.

Margaret was wrong. Drowsily, she drove down the seedy, poorly lit avenue, then stopped for a traffic light behind the only other car in view. Almost immediately, all four doors opened, and Margaret saw three young men get out of the three passenger seats. Slowly they started toward her, menacing, terrifying.

Margaret's heart started to pound. Her doors were unlocked! And for the life of her, she couldn't remember where the automatic switch was!

Everything seemed to click into slow motion, "as if a record or movie had been slowed down," Margaret says. Wildly she considered putting the car in reverse or speeding up to run over them. But she seemed paralyzed with fear. "God help me...." It was all Margaret could think to murmur.

Instantly two enormous headlights shone right behind her, as if a huge eighteen-wheeler had pulled up inches from her rear bumper. The lights beamed through her car and seemed to flood the entire avenue with a radiant white glow. Margaret looked at the storefronts, the parking lot several yards ahead—everything was bathed with brilliance.

Yet how could that be! For she had heard no truck approaching, no sound of an engine revving or shifting gears. And despite the powerful glare behind her, the night was completely hushed.

At that moment the driver emerged from the car in front of Margaret and also started toward her. *God, please!* she prayed. She was going to die here—she knew it. Then, incredibly, Margaret saw a look of shock, fear, terror replace the young man's threatening expression. "He put his hands way up, almost in a gesture of apology toward the light," Margaret says, "and backed up right into the car." The others jumped in, and the car sped off, tires squealing around the next corner.

Margaret slumped against the seat, almost weeping in relief. It had all happened so fast! Had it been a dream? But no, the headlights were still there. Slowly she stepped on the gas and pulled away from the corner.

The twin beacons followed her, illuminating the night in a glow that was almost...heavenly. Margaret began to feel serene, protected, almost blessed. And yet there wasn't a sound behind her.

When she reached a forested area, she saw the lights silently turn off to the left and disappear. Just a few blocks more and she was safely home. "I was shaking, almost a holy trembling, and my husband knew something important had happened," Margaret remembers. She told him of her close call.

"Where did you say the truck turned off?" Bob asked.

"Right at the woods," Margaret described the scene. Bob shook his head. "It did, Bob," she insisted. "I saw it go left."

There was a look of wonder on Bob's face. "Margaret, nothing could turn there. There's no road anywhere near the woods."

No one can explain how things like this happen, but they do. At these moments the invisible world that exists all around us shows itself briefly. In the following chapters you will find more real life stories of people whose lives were affected by that world.

～

While mortals sleep, the angels keep
Their watch of wondering love.

—PHILLIPS BROOKS (1835–93)

To Protect and Bear Us Up

They [his angels] shall bear thee up in their hands,
lest thou dash thy foot against a stone.

—Psalm 91:12

An Angel on Board

I HAD FLOWN MY PLANE to Eirunepe in the Amazon, to minister in the church located there. It was a six-hour flight from Manaus. The next day I headed back home to Manaus, alone. I was flying the plane heading 60 degrees from north, and feeling rather tired, I dozed. While I slept, it seemed I saw a man flying the plane. He had four markers on his shoulder, signifying his rank as captain. He was holding the double control and looking straight ahead. When I finally came out of my drowsy stupor, the plane was headed straight and level as a tabletop. It had not gone up or down, leaned to one side, flown in circles or crashed. It was perfectly level and was still flying at 60 degrees. I do not know how long I slept, but God sent an angel to fly my plane and take care of me.

Bennie DeMerchant
Missionary in Brazil

THE BLINDED TERRORISTS

During Holy Week of 1984, the United Pentecostal Church International of El Salvador held a national convention in the National Gymnasium at San Salvador. Rev. and Mrs. Keith Clark from America were the special speakers of the convention.

These were the days when El Salvador was in the throes of civil war. One night toward the close of the service, armed terrorists came into the building and started asking people questions. One of the ushers overheard the terrorists asking the people to point out where the North Americans were, for they wanted to kidnap and kill them. Keith Clark was on the platform, speaking in English, with bright lights shining on him, while I was interpreting into Spanish with my American accent.

We noticed that the terrorists would talk to one person, look towards the platform and then go talk to another person. Suddenly we all realized that something supernatural was going on. All the people, several thousand of them, could see us, but the terrorists could not. They looked at the platform, but their eyes were blinded to the North Americans who were there. God sent His angels to protect us that night from the terrorists' cruelty and murder.

Bruce Howell
Missionary in El Salvador

THE MAN WITH THE LUNCHBOX

It had been reckless of me, taking a before-dawn stroll through the tangle of streets behind the Los Angeles bus terminal. But I was a young woman arriving in the great city for the first time. My job interview was five hours away, and I couldn't wait to explore.

Now I'd lost my way in a Skid Row neighborhood. Hearing a car pass, I turned and, in the flash of light, saw three men lurking behind me, trying to keep out of sight in the shadows. Trembling with fright, I did what I always do when in need of help. I bowed my head and asked God to rescue me.

But when I looked up, a fourth man was striding toward me in the dark! *Dear God, I'm surrounded.* I was so scared, it took me a few seconds to realize that even in the blackness I could *see* this man. He was dressed in an immaculate workshirt and denim pants, and carried a lunchbox. He was about thirty, well over six feet. His face was stern but beautiful (the only word for it).

I ran up to him. "I'm lost and some men are following me," I said in desperation. "I took a walk from the bus depot—I'm so scared."

"Come," he said. "I'll take you to safety."

He was strong and made me feel safe.

"I...I don't know what would have happened if you hadn't come along."

"I do." His voice was resonant, deep.

"I prayed for help just before you came."

A smile touched his mouth and eyes. We were nearing the depot. "You are safe now."

"Thank you—so much," I said fervently.

He nodded. "Good-bye, Euphie."

Going into the lobby, it hit me. *Euphie!* Had he really used my first name? I whirled, bust out onto the sidewalk. But he had vanished.

Euphie Eallonardo
Guideposts

THE ANGEL WHO PUT MY CAR IN REVERSE

The first of December, 1997, I was taking my son Timothy to get a haircut. We stopped at a red-light, and there were quite a few cars behind me. When the light turned green, I looked both ways and didn't see anything, so I started across the intersection.

My son was looking to my left and saw a car coming towards us at sixty or seventy miles an hour. "Mom," he cried with great intensity.

"What?" I said with the same intensity. At the same time I put on my brakes just as the car flew right past us. I sat there trembling, knowing how close we came to having an accident.

"Mom you can go now," Timothy said.

I put my foot on the gas, but the car backed up instead of going forward. I looked down and saw that the gearshift was in reverse—but I hadn't put it in reverse. I had to change gears so we could drive off.

God had sent an angel to back me up out of the way of the speeding car of death. He also prevented me from backing into the cars behind me when I put my foot on the gas, because I had really stepped on the gas to go on across the intersection. My son and I both knew that we were saved from a serious accident, and we felt as though God had sent His angel to protect us. Shaken but grateful, we went on to the barbershop, praising God for sparing us from a tragic accident.

Brenda Aguirre
Stockton, California

THE UNDERWATER ANGEL

When Dino Lambropolis was a little boy, Nazi Germany was ruling Greece. The Greeks experienced great poverty and hunger and many people were starving. Homes and hospitals were destroyed. One day Dino went down to the wharf to see if he could find some food.

"Can you swim little boy?" a Nazi soldier asked him.

"No," said Dino.

Laughingly the soldier picked him up and threw him into the sea. Dino went down and came up twice gasping for air. The third time he went down he knew he was drowning. It was then he saw a white light, looking like an angel, under the water. It came towards him and enveloped him. He then shot upward out of the water and was at the other end of the wharf away from the Nazi soldier.

He was so shocked by his experience that he could not talk for two weeks. In wonderment he thought many times about the supernatural deliverance from drowning and knew that God had a special purpose for his life.

This incident was related by Joan Ewing

GUARDS ON THE ROOFTOP

Bill Thompson, a missionary to Colombia for over thirty years, once spent the night in a small, primitive farmhouse in the mountains above a village. He was awakened the next morning by a man inspecting the outside of the house.

"Where are the connections for the lights?" the man asked.

"What lights do you mean?" Thompson responded. "There are none here."

"Last night, some hired killers were sent from the village to harm you," the man confessed. "But they saw guards on the roof with bright spotlights, so they did not come near. Where are the wires that powered the lights?"

It was then the missionary's pleasure to tell the villager about God and His guardian angels.

Taken from *Search for Truth*

THE GUARDIAN ANGEL

Sunday, January 18, 1998, I was driving home from Costco in Sherman Oaks, California, and stopped at a red-light at a very busy intersection. The light turned green and I was the first car to move out. In the middle of the intersection I heard a horn honk and instinctively slammed on my brakes. A car that seemed to be flying came from the left and swerved around me, doing at least fifty miles an hour, missing me by inches. After the car had passed me (it was like a blur), I turned my head to look and saw that it was a white Corvette.

There was a stunned moment during which none of the other motorists moved as everybody realized how close we had been to having a terrible accident. The man next to me looked as though he was about to have a stroke, he was so shook up because he would also have been involved in the crash. Tears filled my eyes as I realized I was the one who would have taken the brunt of the impact. The Corvette would have hit directly into the driver's side where I was sitting. It all happened so quickly. If he had not honked, if I had not stopped immediately, and if God had not been watching over me, I would have been lying bloody and mangled in a pile of twisted steel.

As I made my way home I realized that I had never been more close to death or serious injury than at that moment. Immediately after arriving home I called my mother. She told me she had had a burden for me all day, and had told my father that she had felt a heaviness for me. She went to the back of the house where there are big windows, looked up into the heavens and specifically prayed, "God send your guardian angels to protect Sherrie today."

I will never forget how close to death I was and how God sent His angels to protect me in answer to my mother's prayer.

Sherrie Woodward
Sherman Oaks, California

THE BRONZE CAPE

One Wednesday evening after work, after getting off the bus, I was making my way up a very steep, rugged hill on the outskirts of our city of Porto Alegre, Rio

Grande do Sul, Brazil. Some friends were having a church meeting at their house at the top of the hill. The darkness made it difficult to climb the hill. There were boulders in my pathway and it was hard to find the pathway; there were no roads, just paths.

At one point I saw a group of young people standing around buying and selling drugs and using them openly. The men in this rough place were armed with guns and knives. When I tried to pass by two young people, they pointed a gun at my face and brandished a knife at me, but I kept walking, even though I wasn't sure just where it was I was going. I thought of turning around and going home, but something kept me from doing that. I knew I was in a lot of danger. *Maybe I acted foolishly in coming to this place at this time of night*, I thought.

I could tell the young people were thinking of doing harm to me. I prayed desperately, "Señor, don't let me die in this place." A little farther along I suddenly saw coming down from heaven a huge angel. He had a cape of bronze in his hands and he threw it over me. The cape surrounded me and covered me completely, without my feeling its weight on my body. Yet, I knew that even if someone would stick a knife through me, I would not feel a thing, since the angel had put this protective cape over my body.

I continued walking through several more areas just as rough as the one I have described, but no one could touch me. I had God's protection. I also found the path I was looking for. As I reached the top of the hill a young girl came out of her house and said, "Come into our home where we are having service." From that small beginning, there now stands a great church on that hill, on the very spot where the services were being held that night.

Valdenir P. Torma
Porto Alegre, Brazil

AN ANGEL SWIMMING UNDERWATER

On October 1, 1996, my son Mike, his wife Karen and their two children
Austin and Alexa were staying in our home while I was in Missouri attending my
mother's funeral. Randy, my husband, along with Karen and the children were at
home enjoying a normal day, while Mike was on his way home from work.

Austin, then four, and Alexa, then three, were playing in the backyard. When
Karen went to check on them, they were gone. She alerted Randy; they
searched the house and the side yards for them without success. Then they
noticed a board missing in the back fence leading to a neighbor's yard. Running
next door, they discovered the children in the neighbor's swimming pool. Austin
was already lying on the bottom of the pool, and Alexa was about a foot from
the bottom.

Jumping into the pool, Randy pulled Alexa out by the back of her clothes,
brought her up, and put her on the side of the pool. Then he went back after
Austin, he brought him up and started CPR. Alexa started coughing up water, but
Austin had no pulse, and Randy couldn't revive him. In the meantime, Karen had
called 911. The police, the emergency response team, a fire rescue squad and TV
reporters and cameramen were all present when Mike drove up. The children were
rushed to San Jose Hospital, where they were admitted to ICU.

Randy reached our pastor's wife, Sharon Nelson, at home. She went to the
church and told her husband, John Nelson, about the tragedy. As God would
have it, the choir at the church was practicing. They immediately went to prayer
for Austin and Alexa. Mike and Karen were praying in the emergency room
also. They were especially concerned about Austin, who was in a light coma.
But as Mike was praying, God told him that the children would be okay.

After Mike and Karen had been taken by security to the blue room, a waiting
room for families of critically ill and dying patients, a specialist came in. He said

that both children could possibly have respiratory distress for as long as the next thirty days, and he was almost positive that they would have pneumonia. He also said that because they were under the water more than five minutes, they would probably have permanent brain damage. They had been in the water for over seven minutes! He said there was nothing to do but wait.

Shortly thereafter, Austin woke up and wanted his mama. Both children were released within twenty-four hours. The doctor who had taken care of Alexa checked her lungs before she was released. "Her lungs sound like brand new lungs," she said.

Austin started kindergarten in 1997 and Alexa turned four in December 1997. Alexa told us later that there was "an angel" swimming under the water with them. They never did get pneumonia, nor did they suffer any brain damage. Today they are perfectly healthy.

Randy, my husband, had refused to go to my mother's funeral with me, and I couldn't understand why. He just kept saying, "I can't go. I don't know why, but I just can't go." The evening he called me to tell me about the accident, he said with tears in his voice, "God kept me here to save our grandbabies. I pulled them out of the water, but God did the rest."

Jeannie Pearson
San Jose, California

ANGELS IN THE FIRE

On December 22, 1987, in Harvey Station, New Brunswick, Canada, after a hectic day of Christmas preparations, our family had all gone to bed. Shortly after midnight, I was awakened by the smell of smoke and then a loud swirling, gushing sound. Throwing my arm across my husband David, I screamed, "Honey, the house is on fire!"

We jumped out of bed and ran to the stairway, but the smoke and heat were so unbearable it was impossible to go downstairs. Fear and panic struck us. Our ten-year-old daughter, Amy Beth was sleeping on the first floor of our home. We then ran across the hall and grabbed our eight-year-old son, Chadwick, and rushed to his window, knowing this was our only way out.

My husband dropped our son down first, then he and I both jumped from the second story, all of us in our bed clothes and bare feet. There was a drift of snow to break our fall, so none of us broke any bones. We were on our feet instantly, running to the nearest window and door, hoping one might be unlocked. Every minute counted knowing that Amy Beth was inside the house in the horrible heat and smoke.

David began to pound on her window and shout her name, trying to use his bare hands to break through. Being desperate for help, I hailed a truck on the highway in front of our house. The two men later told us they weren't going to stop, thinking it was a marital dispute seeing me in my night gown and bare feet. But one said, "We'd better stop because the lady seems so desperate." They took a shovel and helped my husband break the second pane of glass and a set of grills out of the window.

Thick, black smoke billowed out of the bedroom window. One of the men said, "We can't go in there."

But the love of a father said, "Oh, yes we can. We *have* to go in there." David climbed in the window and found Amy Beth. But when he tried to lift her, he felt himself being overcome by the thick smoke and sickening fumes. Right at that moment he felt a presence and strength help him lift her and hand her out the window to the men waiting outside. He then managed to climb out himself. When he got to Amy Beth, the only sign of life was a faint moan.

Our whole family was taken to the hospital, but Amy Beth did not regain consciousness until the following day. We feel that her speedy recovery was because of what happened in another city.

In the community of Ripples, New Brunswick, where we had formerly lived, there was an elderly woman who was known to be a mighty prayer warrior. Her name was Violet Flowers. She also was awakened shortly after midnight, feeling a heavy burden for our family, though she did not know what was taking place in our lives. Putting wood in her kitchen stove, she sat in her rocking chair all night long and prayed for us. Her burden of prayer did not lift until midafternoon the following day. I credit Amy Beth's complete recovery to her earnest prayers.

I believe with all my heart that God placed angels in the bedroom beside my husband and helped him and Amy Beth to get out of our burning home. He brought us through the fire without a burn or broken bone. What could have been a fatal tragedy was turned into a miracle because someone cared enough to pray for us when they felt a premonition of danger.

Grace Ann Gee
Quebec, Canada

ASK FOR WOODY

My best friend, Merietha, called just before five. "There's a big sale at Macy's," she said. "I'll meet you at the subway after work." I wasn't in the mood for an excursion all the way from Brooklyn, N.Y., into Manhattan, but Merietha was partially paralyzed on her left side, and though she got around well with her cane, it was easier for her to move through the throngs of shoppers with my help.

By the time we were done at Macy's it was after nine. The subway wasn't the best place at night for two ladies bogged down with packages, so we decided to take it only as far as a stop where we could transfer to a bus to Brooklyn. Still, I was worried. I prayed as we got on the train, *Lord, help us have a safe trip home.*

When we pulled into a station on the Lower East Side, Merietha gathered her bags and headed for the doors. "I think our stop is the next one," I said tentatively. "No, this is it," she insisted. As soon as we got up to the street I knew we were in the wrong place. Not a soul in sight. Peering around the corner, I spotted a bus stop beneath a lamppost about five blocks away.

We started in that direction. Then, from out of the darkness, a voice called, "Mrs. Carroll!" A young man I had never seen before came up to us.

"Mrs. Carroll," he said, "what are you two doing out here at this time of night? It's not safe."

I glanced at his shabby jeans and T-shirt. "Do I know you?" I asked, hoping my voice sounded steady. When I felt Merietha's grip on my arm tighten, I looked at the man more closely. I couldn't help but notice his deep brown eyes, which seemed full of concern and compassion.

"Where are you from?" I asked. He walked along with us, going slowly so Merietha could keep up, but didn't offer any information about himself.

Near the bus stop a group of surly-looking people blocked our path. They glared menacingly, but our companion remained calm. "Hi, folks," he said. "These ladies are with me." They let us pass.

The bus came, and the young man rode with us back to Brooklyn. Before we said good-bye I gave him my phone number. "Stay in touch," I urged. "I'd like to keep you in my prayers."

He smiled. "Ask for Woody," he said, handing me his number.

The next day I called to thank him properly. "This is a boarding house," the person who answered told me. "No one by that name lives here."

Then where had Woody come from? Suddenly I knew. After all, hadn't I asked the Lord to help us get home safely?

Mildred V. Carroll
Brooklyn, New York
Guideposts

Around our pillows golden ladders rise,
And up and down the skies,
With winged sandals shod,
The angels come and go, the Messengers of God!

—RICHARD HENRY STODDARD (1825–1903)

To Bring Messages of Hope and Healing

And there appeared an angel unto him from heaven, strengthening him.

—LUKE 22:43

&

THE ETHIOPIAN ANGEL

UR GRANDDAUGHTER, ASHLEY, was born September 5, 1987, with a serious medical condition: transposition of the great arteries. This means that the arteries do the opposite of what they are supposed to do. The oxygenated blood goes into the lungs and the blue blood goes into the body. Ashley was in Charlottesville, Virginia, at University Hospital. When she was four days old and undergoing a surgical procedure, a doctor's instrument slipped and punctured her heart. This necessitated open heart surgery for her. From that bungled procedure her condition worsened and she was near death several times. We had our church and friends across America pray for a miracle.

After her open heart surgery, she had two chest tubes inserted in both sides of her lungs. When they went to remove them, she inhaled and this caused too much air to enter her lungs. So they could not remove them as planned. It hurt us to see her lying there so helpless lingering between life and death.

One evening after my daughter, Kim, and I went back to the motel where we were staying, we begin to weep profusely, praying and calling on the Lord to help us.

While we were praying, the Lord brought to my mind the time when my husband pastored a church in Canada. It was around 1969. We had heard of a church in Ethiopia who had many members suffering with malaria. Some members had died and all were in dire need. Our church went on a thirty-day period of prayer and fasting for the church in Ethiopia. Some time later one of the leaders of that church sent us a letter. The Lord had shown her, she wrote, that our church was praying for them, and that because of our prayers, the disease was stayed and many lives were spared.

As I remember this incident, I prayed, "Lord, send an Ethiopian angel to come and help us!" My body was weak from crying and praying—we were so desperate for a miracle—but after this prayer I felt peace.

The day finally arrived when they were going to do another surgery to take the tubes out. The nurse told us to go get something to eat while they took Ashley's signs and prepared her for surgery. As Kim and I were walking down the hall, a black man came walking towards us all dressed in white. When he got near us, he smiled, nodded and began to sing Doris Akers' "Sweet, Sweet Spirit."

> "And for these blessings
> We lift our hearts in praise,
> Without a doubt we'll know that we have been revived
> When we shall leave this place."

Kim and I both felt chills all over our bodies as he walked on by us singing. When we turned to thank him, he had disappeared from the long hallway. We looked at one another, hardly able to breathe. "He was an angel," we both said smiling.

When we went back to where Ashley was being prepared for surgery, we started to go in, but the nurse stopped us from entering. "You can't go in yet," she said. "Something has happened." Finally they told us that while the nurse was getting things prepared, after she had strapped the baby down, she turned around and discovered the tubes were out. They had been taped down and there was no way they could have come out except through surgery, because of Ashley's medical problem.

Ashley did not have to have surgery that day. Someone else removed the tubes. God sent his angel to give us a miracle in our night of darkness and despair.

Because of Ashley's condition, she had had three strokes. The doctors said she would be a vegetable, blind and unable to move her limbs, and they told Kim to take her to a neurosurgeon when she was six months old.

On that visit the doctor asked, "Is she able to move her legs and arms?"

"Yes," Kim said.

"By the looks of these X-rays," the doctor said, "the baby should be a vegetable." But after checking Ashley, he said, "You do not need me. This baby is fine."

That has been ten years ago. When she was five years old, Ashley was reading at a fourth-grade level. She is a witness to the miraculous power of God! We will always be grateful for the heavenly visitor he sent to us in the hospital.

Marilyn Turner
Vinton, Virginia

MARCUS'S MIRACLE

Brenda Brown kissed her sixteen-year-old son Marcus good-bye before he opened the car's passenger-side door. She watched him cross Center Street to Edison High and waited until he was safely across. Moments before, she had told him, "Whatever you find in life, God is in charge."

She had no idea how strongly that faith would be challenged. Hours later, after being stricken at an Edison football practice, Marcus Brown slipped into a coma from a brain hemorrhage. For two consecutive nights, doctors told Brenda and her husband, Robert, their son wouldn't survive. But he pulled through. Today Marcus Brown is awake and alert, flashing his trademark sense of humor and warming smile. Every day is a small victory.

He's slowly regaining use of his left side. His memory of certain events is improving, including the near-tragic details of that warm Wednesday afternoon, September 3, 1997, when his life and the lives of his friends and family forever changed.

Brenda Brown, who was shopping across the street from Edison High School when her son collapsed, was paged. She returned the call and was told her son was in the hospital in a coma. "I rushed over there, and when I got there, the doctor told me, 'I'm sorry to have to meet you under such circumstances, but your son is in a coma and on a breathing machine.'" "I didn't cry," Brenda Brown recalls. "I just fell to my knees and started praying." For three days, Marcus grew worse. The doctors said there was almost no chance he would survive the night, and prepared the Brown family for the worst.

Instead of losing hope, Brenda Brown gained resolve. "I just turned to everybody who was there and said, 'It's time for us to start praying.' We all got on our knees and started praying." Brenda herself, who hadn't eaten or slept in three days, finally fell asleep Saturday night in the hospital waiting room. "I wanted to stay up, but I just prayed and went to sleep," she said.

The Browns' only daughter, Sabrina, checked in on her mother. "It was right after the doctors told us there was nothing else they could do," said Sabrina, a twenty-one-year-old student at Delta College. "When everybody left the room, my mom was lying on a couch and just about to fall asleep. I looked, and I saw an angel above her. I couldn't believe what I was seeing, so I left, but when I came back, it was still there. It was a very short man with a beard, wearing a long robe." Sabrina went to her brother and uncle and told them what she saw. When they returned to the room, the lights were out and the angel was gone.

"When I saw the angel, I knew he was going to be OK," Sabrina said.

On Sunday, Marcus's vital signs returned to normal. His blood pressure and brain pressure decreased, his fever was gone, and X-rays showed no cause of the swelling.

Reporter Bob Highfill
The Record newspaper
Friday, October 24, 1997

THE EMERGENCY ROOM ANGELS

In 1988, while I was walking along the riverfront in St. Louis, Missouri, I noticed my heel start to itch and begin to swell very hard and dramatically. Later in the day I removed my shoes, thinking they were the cause of the problem. Other episodes began to take place. A finger would swell up and itch until I couldn't stand it. A big red spot appeared on my arm and began to swell, then my whole body started to swell. I was in the emergency room seven times in one year. It seemed all they wanted to do was to bring in other doctors to look at me because they had never seen anything like it before.

I looked like the inside of a watermelon; my ears looked like clown's ears all blown up. At one time I was lying in my bed for days with the ceiling fan on, the air conditioning on and my sister-in-law packing me with ice. They would send me home from the emergency room and tell me not to take hot showers or baths, and gave me medicine to counteract whatever I might be allergic to. They also sent me to the best allergy doctor in Illinois: Dr. Zimmerman. After much testing, he said I was probably in the 10% group where they never find out what it is.

This was a very traumatic time for me. One day, on a Tuesday, I was so lifeless and weak, I knew that as soon as my husband came home I would have to make another trip to the emergency room, because I could not even change my clothes. When my husband came home from work he took one look at me and wanted to call "911." I said, "No, just put me in the back of the car and take me to the emergency room." When I got there, they took one look at me and went into action. From having worked at a hospital before, I knew exactly what was happening; life was leaving me.

The room filled with specialists and doctors. They could hardly get blood from me because my arms were so full of fluid. I heard a nurse say, "We are losing her, we are losing her."

"Please," I asked God, "send me some angels, now!" Immediately three angels appeared at my right shoulder, a sight I will never forget. They walked around to the foot of the table. They didn't bother anyone and nobody bothered them because no one saw them but me.

The nurse at my left shoulder said, "I wish I could wave a magic wand and make everything O.K."

I said, "That's not necessary. I have God and my angels, and I am fine."

Then I heard a doctor say, "We've got her back."

After they got me stabilized, they called in a specialist from Missouri. He said, "You will never make it to the emergency room next time." They gave me a prescription, a vial of medication, and a syringe to take home. But I have never had to use them!

I will always have the memories of those angels in that emergency room. I'm so thankful that I know God.

Wanda Snyder
Granite City, Illinois

THE HEALING ANGEL

In 1988, I was diagnosed with lymphoma. The doctors termed it aggressive and stage two, and planned aggressive measures of treatment, including several intravenous medications and an additional number of oral medications. I remember the doctors saying, "We must hit it hard and hit it fast if we have a hope of winning this battle through chemotherapy."

Like so many other cancer patients, I bloated, lost my hair, and my personality had severe mood swings, but my faith in God was stable. One night about four months into treatments, I was suffering severely and couldn't sleep. Lying in my bed, I suddenly saw a figure walk down the hall of my house, a man so large that he stooped to avoid touching the ceiling with his head. He came over to the bed where I lay and put two massive hands on my chest. Instantly his contact felt like electrical regeneration. Although the current created by his touch seemed to vibrate my whole body from head to foot, it neither awoke my wife, nor had any kind of adverse effect on me. For about two to three minutes he stood over me with a confident expression on his face and healing comfort in his hands. Then without saying a word, he turned as though he would walk away and vanished before my very eyes.

Carroll McGruder
Kennett, Missouri

THE GLOWING ANGEL

Jackie is a beautiful girl of seventeen with shining black hair and sparkling brown eyes. A delightful glow sets her apart from other beautiful young girls.

Three years ago Jackie faced a painful tragedy. Doctors had discovered a tumor on her cheekbone....It had spread its deadly tentacles throughout the entire cheek region of her attractive face. Surgery offered the only hope for Jackie's life. The doctors would be making an incision along the nose area and down through the upper lip. All the teeth on the left side of her face would have to be removed as well as the cheekbone, the nose bone, and the jaw bone. Needless to say, an operation of this immensity, performed on the face of a lovely, at that time fourteen-year-old girl, was a grim prospect. Many tears were shed.

Several days before the surgery, lying in her hospital bed, she thought about what it would mean to go through life so terribly scarred, if indeed she even lived through the operation. She was frightened, she desperately wanted to live. She wanted to experience all that life held for her. As she tossed on her pillow in lonley fear that night, she began to pray. With tears of anxious apprehension, she asked God to help her.

About two o'clock in the morning Jackie was awakened. She didn't know what woke her up; she only knew she was awake and alert. She saw a glowing light at the foot of her bed, and the silvery form of an angel appeared. The presence was very powerful and totally loving. An aura of stillness filled Jackie like the warmth of a summer day. She felt enfolded by the preence and a sense of incredible wonder touched every part of her body.

A voice filled with sunshine said, "Do not be afraid, Jackie. You are going to be all right." And then the angel presence was gone.

The following day, Jackie was taken to the X-ray room for preoperative X-rays. To the utter astonishment of the doctors, every trace of the tumor and its deadly tentacles was gone!

Taken from *When Angels Appear*
by Hope MacDonald

The Doctor Who Kept Watch

The first thing I noticed that morning in my fiancé's hospital room was the chair close to his bed. *That's odd,* I thought. I knew the chair hadn't been there when I had left well after the end of visiting hours the night before.

Twenty-four hours earlier it had been a beautiful, sunny day when John and I went for a long bike ride. John had lost control on a rough patch of road and fallen hard onto the asphalt. At the hospital a neurosurgeon and a plastic surgeon examined John while I paced outside the treatment room.

Finally the doctors let me in to see him. John looked weak and pallid.

"He has a bad concussion," one of the specialists told me.

"There's nothing more we can do right now," said the second. "Go home and try to get some sleep."

I sat by John's side for a few hours. Then, before I left, I prayed, "Dear Lord, please watch over him tonight."

This morning John looked so much better; the color had come back to his face and he seemed more relaxed. As I stood by his bed, he woke up, smiling, alert. We talked about the accident.

"Thank goodness for those three doctors," he said.

"Three?" I wondered aloud.

"Yes, there was a doctor with a beard who watched over me all night. He sat right in that chair."

I looked at the chair. And I knew my prayer had been answered.

Sue McCusker
Canton, Georgia
Guideposts

THE ANGEL CAME ON WEDNESDAY

Until that incredible morning, I thought that angels were something you saw on Christmas cards or read about in the Bible. I never conceived of them as beings who could step into our lives.

Seventeen years ago my life was in terrible turmoil. At 44, I had recently been diagnosed with uterine cancer. I agonized over the possibility that I might leave my four children motherless. My husband, Gary, a strapping former Air Force master sergeant, was devastated. He had lost his first wife to the same type of cancer. He took me in his arms and with tears streaming down his face said, "I can't bear the thought of losing you."

My doctor scheduled a radical hysterectomy for later in the month at Cape Fear Valley Hospital. Meanwhile, Gary and I did the only thing we could—we prayed. Every day we knelt together and asked God to heal me, to give us time to raise our children. Friends and fellow members of the Haymount United Methodist Church prayed for me as well. We had everyone we knew praying. But as the surgery date loomed, I felt my faith begin to waver. What lay ahead seemed so frightening. I knew God was a healer, but I didn't know anyone who had ever been healed.

It was the Wednesday before I was to enter the hospital. Gary and I got up and ate breakfast. Again we prayed together.

At about 10 o'clock, as Gary was doing some chores around the house and I worked on bills at my desk in the solarium in our front foyer, the doorbell rang. Gary answered it. When he opened the door I heard a deep, melodious voice say, "I've come to tell Ann."

I turned to see a tall black man standing on the doorstep. He was taller than my six-foot-five-inch husband. His skin was ebony and his eyes were a deep, shimmering azure. He looked past Gary and fixed his gaze directly on me. "Ann," he said, "the cancer in your body has been healed."

"How do you know?" I managed to gasp.

"God told me," he answered.

I stared at him uncomprehendingly. I noticed his unusual clothing. He wore a loose, black, gossamer tunic with swirling golden threads, and dark, flowing trousers. His shoes were woven from some ribbonlike material. He was clean-shaven with close-cropped hair, and there was an aura of peace about him.

"Would you like to come in?" I said. I glanced at Gary, who was as awestruck as I. He stepped aside for the man to enter.

"Sir," I said, standing up, "I don't understand....What is your name?"

He smiled radiantly and touched his left shoulder with the index and middle finger of his right hand. "My name is Thomas."

Speaking in the most comforting tones, Thomas told me I must not worry. He quoted Isaiah: "... and with his stripes we are healed." And then he said, "Before I go, I must pray for you."

He held out his right palm about 12 inches from my forehead. "Father God," he began, and as he prayed I felt intense heat radiating from his hand. My legs weakened, my eyes closed and as I fell gently to the floor I was aware of a powerful white light moving up through my body.

I awoke to see Gary leaning over me. "Ann, are you all right?"

"Where is he?" I asked.

But Thomas had vanished.

I crawled to the phone and called my doctor. "Something has happened to me that I can't explain," I said. "I won't need the surgery."

The doctor said he realized how the stress and fear could be affecting my imagination. But I insisted. Finally we compromised. If I would show up for the surgery, he would perform another biopsy as I lay on the operating table before any further procedures were done.

I agreed. And that Sunday I entered the hospital as planned. When I awoke in my room afterward, my doctor was at my bedside shaking his head. "Ann, I can't explain it. Your tissue appears clean. We didn't operate. We'll do further tests, but for now you're in the clear."

In the years since, there has been no recurrence of the cancer. Thomas did not return. But no longer do I think of angels as confined to Christmas cards. I know that they are here among us, doing God's work in our lives.

Ann Cannady
Fayetteville, North Carolina
Guideposts

❧

When angels come, the devils leave.

—ANCIENT PROVERB

CHAPTER 4

To Send God's Provision

Be not forgetful to entertain strangers: for thereby
some have entertained angels unawares.

—HEBREWS 13:2

∾

A SPECIAL DELIVERY

OR SEVERAL YEARS I WORKED as a cook/supervisor of a large military day care center in Germany. I was in desperate need of a very large stainless steel pot with large handles and a good fitting lid. In order to cook enough food like soup, chicken, or chili, for the children and staff I had to use several small pots, which took up valuable burners on the stove. I asked my director if it was possible to purchase a large pot for the kitchen. When she inquired about it, she was told it could not be ordered at that time, possibly because it was a very expensive item. I was thankful to the Lord for the pots I had to cook with, but I still greatly desired a large pot.

One day, about two weeks after my supervisor inquired about the pot, an old German workman came into the center carrying a large beat-up box for my director. I was at the cashier's desk at the time, and I remember one of the workers signing a wrinkled paper the man brought with him. We placed the unopened box on the director's desk, not knowing what it contained. Later, the director called me into her office. "Do you know what's in the box?" she asked.

"No, I don't," I told her.

She then opened the box and showed me its contents—a stainless steel pot with large handles and a tight lid, the most wonderful pot I had ever seen! "You might as well use it, since it's here," she told me.

Neither of us had any idea where it came from. Several weeks later, and after much use of that wonderful pot, my supervisor told me that no one could find out who had ordered it and also that no one had paid for it.

The pot was just what I needed and was a tremendous answer to prayer. Was it sent as a gift from God and hand-delivered by an angel? I believe it was! While I was at the day care center I used that very special gift every day.

Nancy Hunt
Stockton, California

Two Angels and a Truck out of Nowhere

In 1991, I was driving my car and pulling a trailer full of religious books from San Francisco to Indiana. About 3:00 A.M. in the middle of the desert, my transmission exploded into flames. Immediately I pulled over to the side of the road, jumped out of the car and began to run. In the desert I could see for miles but there were no lights from houses or cars in the surrounding darkness. Then I began to pray, knowing I was stranded with no one in sight to help me.

Suddenly a big truck appeared out of nowhere and pulled up near my car. The driver got out, went over to the car and put the fire out. I was amazed. Then he came over to me and said, "All things work for best. I will help until everything is completed and you are back on the road again with your books."

The driver was as good as his word. He not only called a tow truck, paying the towing fee for the thirty-minute ride back to Reno, Nevada, he drove back with me and paid for my breakfast there. He was an elderly man with white hair and well dressed for a truck driver, but he did not talk much. He stayed with me until the Oldsmobile dealership opened and waited until they told us what it would cost to have the car fixed.

Then the man looked at me, shook my hand, and said these words to me, "God bless you. I will pray that you make it to Indiana and back home to San Francisco safely. I have to go now." But I had never told him where I was going, or where I was from! And he had known without my telling him that I had books in the trailer.

As he walked out of the dealership, I remembered that I had never said thanks for all he had done for me from 3:00 A.M. to 9:15 A.M., so I ran out of the building after him. He was nowhere to be found! It was impossible for him to back that truck out of where it was and be gone that quickly. Then suddenly I realized there had been no name or numbers on that truck, and I began to cry. I did not care who was looking, for I knew God had sent an angel to help me where there was no help to be found.

The second part of the miracle was what happened after this. It cost me $2,100.00 to have the car fixed, a sum I did not have. When I arrived back home and received my bank statement, I discovered a large deposit of $2,500.00 in my account, which I had not made. When I spoke to the manager, who was a good friend of mine, and asked her about what happened in my account, she would not explain it over the phone. "Mr. Spencer," she said, "you have to come in and talk to me."

In the bank, she told me, "Sit down. I can't explain this standing up." I looked at her hands and they began to shake. She then told me the story.

One day during lunch time, a lot of people came in at the same time. She only had two tellers on duty, so she went to help them. As she opened her window, she saw the most beautiful elderly man standing there. He had beautiful white hair and a complexion of light gold skin, with not a wrinkle on it. She explained to me the best she could, the feeling that went all through her body. "It was like being transferred to another world," she said. The man looked at her and handed her a pile of bills—all in hundreds and fifties.

"I'd like to deposit $2,500.00 into Mr. James Spencer's account," he told her, and gave her the account number. (It was impossible for anyone else to know this.)

"When he pushed the money up to me," the manager said, "my fingers touched his and I felt a jolt of electricity whirl through my body. I took the money, and put it in a separate drawer, but when I turned he was gone completely out of the bank."

She asked one of the tellers, "Did you see a beautiful white-haired elderly man at my window?"

The girl said, "No."

She turned to the other teller, a young man, and asked the same question. He too answered no. She then beckoned to the next people in line, a couple, and asked them if they had seen the man at her window. They also said no one was there.

"Before this happened," she told me, "I was an atheist. But this experience has let me know there is a God out there who has angels working for Him on behalf of His children."

James Spencer
Stockton, California

THE FOLDED SHEETS

The story I am going to tell took place when we did not have much money. My husband, Larry, and I and our two children were returning home to Stockton one night from San Diego and decided to stop at a favorite restaurant in Los

Angeles for dinner. We couldn't really afford to eat there, but we wanted to very badly because it had been nearly five years since our last visit. But when we arrived it was nearly eleven o'clock and the restaurant was closing.

"Do you want to take the food to go," the manager asked.

That seemed disappointing, so we said no. We didn't want to spend that much money just to eat in our car and have our seventy-five-pound Doberman drooling on our food.

Seeing our disappointment, the manager offered to give us one of the dinners for free. So we gladly accepted. Sitting down to wait for the free dinner, we began to tell him about how we had enjoyed eating there nearly every day while we were on business trips to Los Angeles. I guess he must have been impressed because he personally packaged two pot roast dinners, two salads, bread, coffee and desserts for us. We could barely carry it all. When we tried to pay, he refused to let us. So we sat outside our favorite restaurant and ate while our children slept in the car. Praise God!

After dinner, around midnight, we started driving, with the children still sleeping. Before too long, though, I could tell that my husband was too tired to drive. I then had a horrible vision of waking up with a paramedic over me and not answering when I kept asking about my little boys. The vision scared me, so I said something to my husband. He pulled over and we rested for a while.

After a brief nap I took over the driving, but I became increasingly tired. I asked the Lord to give me strength, and I sang songs to try and stay awake, but it wasn't working. Remembering my vision, I asked the Lord for strength until I could get to the next city, which was Bakersfield. There we stopped at a motel and I told the man at the desk that I only had twenty-five dollars. I also told him we just needed a few hours to sleep so we could drive home.

He looked at his list of rooms and said, "I have a room upstairs on the end that someone transferred out of, but it's a little messed up. The people complained of some ants in the room. Just bring back the key after you let yourselves in, and leave by nine in the morning before the maids come, and you can have it for free."

When we came to our room, we found only a few little ants in the bathroom. What caught my eye, though, were the crisp sets of folded sheets on the beds. If someone had checked out, they wouldn't have folded up their sheets. And these were brand new sheets. I don't know of any motels that drop off clean sheets to a room at four in the morning, especially when no one is supposed to be in there!

Heather Monteforte
Stockton, California

THE LADY IN WHITE

I am a United States army recruiter. I work in Stockton, California, where my wife and I have lived for twenty-one years. On September 25, 1987, I had to take an applicant to the Greyhound bus station so that he could take a bus to Fresno, California, where he would be inducted into the army. As I saw the bus pull out of the station, I immediately left to go to my car.

It was then I saw an elderly black lady sitting by the side wall, waving at me to come to her. God had sent her to Stockton, she said, and told her that she would find someone in the bus station that needed to be helped. I told her that if she wanted to, she could stay at my house at no charge. She was reluctant at first, but finally agreed to stay.

At the house, I introduced her to my family and told them that she would be staying the night with us. Just as I was leaving to go back to work, she asked, "There is a specific and personal prayer that you have been asking for. What is it?"

In response, I told her my prayer. I wanted to take my wife to the army conference which would be held in Sacramento, but we did not have the finances to go. It would cost us about $150.00 for meals, lodging and transportation for two days.

She then reached inside her bosom and pulled out a handful of $20.00 bills, saying, "God wants me to give you this." It was a total of $200.00. I thanked the lady and left for work. While driving in the car, I thanked God for answering my prayer, while tears ran down my face.

Later, after I came home from work, I shared more conversation with this lady. She was always dressed in white: a white cap over her head, white robe, white shoes. As we were eating dinner, she said, "You don't know if you are entertaining an angel." My wife and I looked at each other, knowing that this was a real angel.

The next morning, I went back to work, but I told my wife to take the lady back to the bus station because she said she had to go to Fresno to help someone else. The lady disappeared out of our life and we never saw her again, but she came after I had prayed a desperate prayer for a specific need.

Pete Lopez
Stockton, California

THE MYSTERIOUS MESSENGER

In December of 1996, our church received word from the escrow company that we needed $30,000 cash within thirty days or else we would lose the property that we had bought a year earlier, planning to build a new church. The reason the escrow took so long was that the company who owned the property sued the bank, and it was in litigation for one year. We had put down $1,000.00 in escrow to hold it. Because of the litigation, we did not have to make a payment for a whole year (this was a blessing in itself).

Needless to say, our small congregation did not have money in excess. We emptied every fund into one large account trying to get the money together. I did not take a salary that month. We put church bills on my own personal credit cards. I called our mortgage company, as well as a few other creditors, and explained that we would not be able to make a payment that month. Things were very tight.

My wife had to take a small job so we could have Christmas for the children and the family. By scraping every penny together, we did just barely close escrow on the 18th. On the 21st, which was a Saturday, I met the treasurer and a trustee's wife at the church, where I told them there was no money to buy gifts and food for all the fatherless and widows of our congregation. This had always been a priority for us. So I told the two women to go buy the gifts and food, and the offering on Sunday would cover it. "Write the checks today," I told them. "Tomorrow's offering will cover it."

As soon as I told them to go ahead and buy the gifts, a woman walked into the church sanctuary. "Is there a man named B. J. Wilmoth here?" she asked one of the women. When she was led up to me, she told me "I've been sent from God; I'm supposed to give this to you," and she handed me a folded piece of paper. I shook her hand, thanked her and she walked out. She did not linger.

I looked down at the folded piece of paper. It was a check for $3,000.00! We ran outside to thank the woman, but she had disappeared. There was no one in sight.

We went back inside and began to praise the Lord, with tears rolling down our cheeks. I told the women, "Go and buy what you need. We have the money." The $3,000.00 also paid our mortgage and car payments for that month.

One month later, the church that had bought our old building (we are now leasing a building, while waiting to build our own), called and said, "You will have all your money in two months," even though the contract stated that they had five years to pay it off. All the months of sacrifice were rewarded richly by unexpected messages, which were orchestrated by God.

I will never forget this time in our life when our budget was stretched so thin.

We did not have one penny, yet we were going on faith to buy things to give to the widows and fatherless. And suddenly $3,000.00 was placed in my hands by a mysterious messenger who said she was sent from God!

Rev. B. J. Wilmoth
Redlands, California

THE INVISIBLE MESSENGER

I had been in the hospital with the disease Lupus, and had not been able to work for about two months. With all the added expenses, I was unable to pay my rent, and I didn't know what to do. I was weak in my body and felt so alone. I had no family in Stockton, California, where I lived, and I did not want to be a bother to other people. Although my friends had been so good to me, helping me with groceries and other necessities, I didn't want to ask them to help with my rent.

So one evening I knelt down and began to pour my heart out to the Lord God, calling out to him in desperation. While I was praying, the doorbell rang. When I opened the door (I know this sounds strange), an envelope just sort of flew into the room. I picked it up, then looked outside. There was nobody that I could see. I begin to get chills and goose bumps, knowing that envelopes just don't fly by themselves.

When I opened the envelope, in it were crisp, brand new bills with the exact amount of my rent payment. The money was wrapped in a white sheet of paper with these words typed on it, "I have been young, and now am old; yet have I not seen the righteous forsaken, nor his seed begging bread" (Psalm 37:25). Beyond a doubt, I knew that God had sent an angel with the rent money in answer to my prayers, and a personal note from his Word to me in my time of extreme need.

Doris Rome
Stockton, California

THE WHITE-COATED ANGEL

Things did not always go well financially for us. Once, when Jerry was pastoring a small church we seemed to come to the end of our resources because of several things that happened in the church. We had been living in a lovely home and driving a fine automobile, but now we found ourselves unable to pay our basic bills. I had always believed that Christians who live by faith should pay their bills on time and thus live beyond reproach, yet our mortgage was three months in arrears; we were being threatend with the disconnection of the utilities, and we had been unable to pay the latest telephone bill. We had reached the stage where we didn't even have a loaf of bread or a box of salt in the house.

We cried out to God in great distress: "God, we stood up for the principles in your Word, and the people have stopped supporting us. Please help us, We don't know what to do."

When we went to church on Sunday, the attendance seemed quite good, and we were hopeful that there would be a decent offering from which our salary could be paid, but we were disappointed. It was the smallest offering the church had ever received since we had been there. That day we returned home with sinking hearts. If things did not improve soon, we would be unable to feed our children, and the house would be repossessed. We had never been in such a serious situation before—at least in this land of plenty.

We prayed earnestly to God that evening: "God, please hear us. Our testimony in the community will be ruined. You know this whole situation has only arisen because we have tried to be faithful to your Word. Lord, provide for our children. Please help us."

The next day I backed the car out of the garage and drove down the road to the supermarket to spend the last twenty dollar bill we had left. As I reached a certain stop sign, I felt as if God was saying to me, "Gail, I want you to praise me."

I would like to be able to say that I immediately responded and began to worship, secure in the knowledge that God would not let us down. Instead I was cross. "Lord, this is not fair. Every time we stand up for what is right we have to go through all this painful persecution. I can't praise you right now."

I continued to moan and complain like the children of Israel in the wilderness, but God said to me once again, "Gail, praise me." I pretended that I had not heard and kept going.

When God spoke to me for the third time, I did begrudgingly begin to praise him, although it was only lip service and not from my heart. Slowly, however, something began to stir within me, and faith in God's power to provide increased. I was able to pray, "Lord, if we do what is right, I know that you will make a way where there seems to be no way. I'm sorry for moaning. Thank you. I know that you are my Provider."

I became so engrossed in praising God that I overshot the turn for the bargain supermarket where I usually purchased my groceries. I stopped in front of another store which was more expensive, but I concluded that since I could only afford a few items, it would not make a significant difference to the bill if I stopped there. Still praising God, I seized my basket and entered the supermarket—totally unaware of the surprises God had prepared for me.

Supermarkets are not generally renowned as locations for the spectacular display of God's power, but that is what took place in that particular store on that particular day. A man in a white meat-cutter's jacket stood inside the door. I noticed that he was picking up one or two items from the shelf and repricing them. I was surprised to discover that a box of salt had been marked down to a penny. Canned hams now only cost a few cents each.

This seemed crazy. The prices I was seeing were ridiculously low. To my amazement I noticed that the man seemed to be repricing all the items I needed most. Drawn as if by a magnet, I followed him up and down the aisles, filling my basket with unbelievably low-priced goods.

"All bread and pastry in this store will be reduced to ten cents for the next five minutes," came an announcement over the loudspeaker. Hardly daring to believe what was happening, I ran over to the shelves and began filling my cart with jelly donuts, cream puffs, large loaves of bread and crusty rolls. This was wonderful!

I managed to find a half gallon of ice-cream marked down to fifty cents. Having a great weakness for coffee, I went to investigate the situation in that department. Sure enough, Mr. White-coat had passed that way with his price-slashing pen, while I had been stocking up on bread and pastries, and I got an unbelievable deal on some coffee.

While I was picking out the coffee, I noticed a small interesting-looking piece of paper lying on the shelf. I picked it up and discovered that it was a coupon which further reduced the price of the coffee, making it virtually free. There were no other coupons in sight, so I concluded that it was probably out of date. Nevertheless, I took it with me to the checkout counter along with my overflowing cart.

As I waited in the line at the checkout counter, I began to panic, fearful that it was somehow a mistake. Some of the items I had taken from the shelves were things I would not normally buy because they were too expensive. Would I now be presented with a bill I couldn't pay?

When it came my turn, the girl looked at the coffee coupon and asked, "Where did you get this?"

"It was on the shelf with the coffee," I said. "Is it valid?"

"Oh, yes, it's valid, but I have never seen one like this before, although I've worked here for years. Were there any more like this?"

"No," I responded, "that seemed to be the only one."

When I pulled out into traffic that day, I had change from my twenty dollars and a back seat loaded with groceries. Needing no prompting now to praise God, I rejoiced at full volume all the way home. "Jerry, come and give me a hand," I called as I started to unload my purchases.

He appeared and gasped as he saw all the bags of provisions I had brought. "Gail, where on earth did you get all this food?" he asked. "You didn't have enough money for a fraction of this." Maybe, fleetingly, he wondered if his wife had done the unthinkable and resorted to shoplifting.

I began to tell him the remarkable story of what had transpired at the supermarket and when I had finished I saw that his eyes were full of tears. "Gail, God sent an angel today to provide for us."

Later that same morning a lady from our church came to visit us. Handing us a large check, she explained that it was the tithe of an inheritance she had recently received. "God told me to give this to you. I was going to wait until Sunday, but he woke me up this morning and told me that you needed it immediately and that I should give it to you today." That check covered our outstanding mortgage payments and all our other unpaid bills. In the space of a few hours all our debts had been cleared and our cupboards were stocked with food.

Gail Rozell
Missionary to Zimbabwe, Africa
Taken from her book *A Reed in His Right Hand*

An angel is a spiritual creature without a body created by God for the service of Christendom and the church.

—MARTIN LUTHER (1483–1546)

CHAPTER 5

To Work with Us in God's Kingdom

And, behold, the angel of the Lord came upon him, and a light shined in the prison, and he...raised him up.

—ACTS 12:7

❧

ANGELS IN CHURCH

Author's note: Once when my husband asked me to speak at Christian Life Center, I prayed and asked God to send His angels to help me. I also asked Him to let someone in the audience see the angels. The following account is from a woman who saw them.

 N JANUARY, 1997, while Joy Haney was ministering in the service, I saw rows of angels standing behind her. They were stair-stepped so I could see each face. There were angels as far as the eye could see. Somehow it seemed there was a greater density of angels behind her on her left, though logically I do not know how that was so.

Their linen-colored robes had gold braid that crisscrossed their chests in the form of an X, and extended to the knee. They were shoeless. Bronze was the tone of their skin and sandy brown the color of their hair. They stood quietly in a somber fashion with arms at their sides. It seemed they were standing guard.

This powerful and electrifying experience left me with "goose pimples," and my hair on my arms standing on end. The feeling of unreality lasted for some hours after. I will never forget the wonderful presence of God that permeated the place, as many were touched by him.

Pam Hanley
Stockton, California

THE FLYING ANGEL

My father, Rev. C. P. Kilgore, was preaching at a brush arbor meeting in Hennepin, Oklahoma, in 1934. One night after the service, the man who had charge of the lanterns that were used in the meeting went to put them up in the little schoolhouse nearby. He felt like something was happening around him, and was very afraid.

Seven of his friends waiting in a car for him saw an angel appear suddenly and follow him. They were dumbfounded and shocked. They watched as he hurridly put the lanterns away then came and joined them in the car. Then he saw the angel! He and his friends, all eight of them watched as the angel went inside the brush arbor, raised his arms and stretched them over the pulpit where my father preached. Then he flew up, skimmed over the top of the building and disappeared.

The occupants in the car went into the small town, riding up and down the streets of Hennepin, waking people up and telling them about what they had just seen. The next night the brush arbor was packed, and there were many healings. A very strong presence of God permeated the meeting that night and every night thereafter for several weeks!

Rev. James Kilgore
Houston, Texas

THE WHITE FORM

In 1994, at Springfield, Missouri, approximately one thousand women were gathered together for a ladies retreat. Joy Haney was the speaker for the event. The first evening as she began to speak, there seemed to be a special presence of the Lord that filled the place. Right in the middle of her message, a woman in the congregation began to have a heart attack. The woman sitting next to her stood to her feet and said, "This woman is having a heart attack. Her arms and chest are hurting and she is in great pain."

Joy Haney had everyone pray for her. When the woman was still in great pain, she told everyone to continue praying. She herself left the platform and started walking down the aisle towards the woman. I happened to look towards the back of the building and noticed the two doors at the entrance. I could see someone all in white, standing by the doors. He slowly started walking down the aisle towards the sick woman. I could not see his face, but I knew this had to be an angel of the Lord.

He reached the place where the circle of women were gathered around the lady praying. Suddenly the sick lady started rejoicing and smiling. The women around her were shouting, "She's all right!" Sister Haney went back to the platform and said, "God's in control of the situation. Everything is fine. God has done a miracle!" The whole congregation of women began to rejoice and shout praises unto God. From that moment on, the Spirit of the Lord fell like rain upon all who were there. We were caught up into the ecstasy of his presence.

I don't know if anyone else saw the angel. Maybe the vision was for me. I was going through some hard things and maybe the Lord showed me that He's in control of all situations.

Darlene Autry
Kennett, Missouri

SHOULDER-TO-SHOULDER ANGELS

On April 2, 1993, I attended a ladies retreat in Alabama. In the conference hall there were huge windows behind the podium that went from the roof to the floor. As Joy Haney ministered to us, my eyes were drawn upward to the windows. I watched in amazement as multitudes of angels lined up from the windows to heaven. I looked away and then back again. They were still there shoulder to shoulder. Again, I looked away, then back; they were still there!

Jesus began to walk down through the two rows of angels! He continued coming and entered into our midst through the window. At that exact moment, Joy Haney stopped and said, "Jesus has entered this place!" There was such an awesome presence of the Lord as he began to minister to the women who were packed into the building!

Kelly Mason
Tigard, Oregon

THE TALL, SHINY ANGEL

When I was eleven, I attended a youth camp in Oklahoma, where we had services in an open tabernacle building. One particular night there was a healing service, and a long line of people came to be prayed for. It was evident that God was healing many of them. Julia, a girl from our church was also there that night.

Julia and I went to the side of the tabernacle and knelt down to pray beside a wall that was about three feet high. On our knees we faced the trees outside, for the tabernacle was built in a clearing in the woods. It was pitch dark in the woods, however, and we couldn't see anything. As I was praying with my head resting on the top of the wall, suddenly the sounds of people praying behind me began to fade out, as if someone had turned the radio down. I found myself moving into a spiritual dimension, where even though I was still inside the tabernacle where everyone was praying, I couldn't hear any sound.

I was so amazed that I lifted my head and opened my eyes. As I looked out into the forest, there, standing among the trees, was a beautiful angel clothed in white, shining very brightly. I couldn't see his face, but he stood very tall and his head reached to the bottom branches of the tallest pine trees. The light shining from him was so bright that all the trees in front of the light seemed to vanish.

The angel stood there for sometime. I don't know how long because I was in a spiritual time zone. The angel began to rise off the ground and slowly disappeared into the trees. I looked above the trees but he wasn't there. As soon as the angel disappeared, I was looking into the dark forest again and couldn't even see the trees it was so dark. Then like someone turned the radio up slowly, I began to hear the people praying again.

Slowly I turned my head to look at Julia. She was looking at me. I said, "Did you see that?"

She said, "You mean the angel?"

"Yes," I said. "I saw it!"

We both cried and rejoiced that God had let us see the angel who had come to be at the healing service that night. It is an experience I will never forget.

Norman Zeno
Stockton, California

THE AUTHORITATIVE ANGEL

My father, C. P. Kilgore, an evangelist in 1925, was once preaching a revival. On one particular occasion, he saw the form of the devil behind him following him into the meeting house. Feeling uneasy, he stopped, and the devil stopped also. He would walk a little further and the devil kept following him. Then suddenly he looked back and the devil was standing still, but was stomping his feet, looking very angry. My father looked in front of him and there stood an angel. The angel was holding up his hand motioning for the devil to leave. The devil had no choice but to obey God's mighty angel. My father walked on inside the building and preached with great power and conviction knowing that God was on his side. What a glorious meeting they had that night.

Rev. James Kilgore
Houston, Texas

THE WARRING ANGEL

It was approximately 3:30 on a Sunday afternoon, in November, 1997. I was reading my Bible in my living room, when suddenly I saw a vision. The vision was of a huge angel standing behind my pastor's wife, Joy Haney. She seemed to be sitting on the floor praying. I later asked the Lord what the meaning of this vision was. He answered me by saying He had sent an angel to keep Satan from interfering with her prayer.

Yoshie H. Brown
Stockton, California

THE GENTLE ANGEL

After receiving a second message on my answering machine from a young woman soliciting business for wedding invitations, I felt impressed to call her. June answered the phone with a cheery hello. I introduced myself and thanked her for the offer, but I had already ordered my invitations, so I declined. When she mentioned her own upcoming wedding, we began to share ideas.

Then she asked some questions about my fiancé and our plans for the future.

I felt impressed to share how God had brought us together and the many blessings He was pouring out upon us. She was so excited to hear what God was doing that she blurted out, "I just have to meet you! I want to hear more about what God is doing!" We made arrangements to meet at the coffee shop in Barnes & Noble Bookstore the next evening, and said our good-byes.

The next day as I was preparing to leave to meet June, I felt impressed to take along my Bible. When we met, it seemed like we knew one other forever, we felt so comfortable together. As we began to talk, I sensed an emptiness inside her and noticed her intense desire to know God better. I opened my Bible and began to show her in the Scriptures that God is a very personal God and that He is very interested in our devotion to Him. Her eyes widened in surprise as we talked. I shared with her my experience of salvation, how I had repented, been baptized and received God's Spirit. She asked question after question, and each time I felt the Lord led me to the answer found in his word.

We were lost in the excitement of our own conversation when a man approached our table, looked at me and said, "You love the Lord, don't you?" I was barely able to answer because his appearance was so breathtaking. He was very tall and slender, and there was a gentleness about him. The light-colored suit he was wearing seemed to glow. His hair was white and his complextion was very fair. He had piercing, sapphire blue eyes like none I had ever seen. His appearance was nothing less than stunning. After stumbling over my answer he spoke some words of reassurance to me. Then he turned to June, my new friend.

"All of what she has told you here tonight is true," he told her. "You are wanting to make a change in your life, and if you will follow the advice you were given you won't be led astray. God really does love you and is concerned about your every need. He knows all about you and He cares." He then pointed to the Bible and said, "All of what has been said here is the truth." His words were filled with compassion and love. Then he simply blessed us and walked away.

Breathless and shaking, we turned to each other. Through my astonishment I managed to say, "That was an angel!"

With eyes as wide as saucers, June simply replied, "I know."

In awe of what had just happened, we both sat quietly for a few moments before saying anything more. With tears welling up in her eyes, June thanked me for coming and sharing with her. I told her that I would be praying for her. Then she said, "I will never forget this evening. I can't believe we actually saw an angel."

Katherine Spacek
Stockton, California

❧

Angels mean messengers and ministers.
Their function is to execute the plan of divine
providence, even in earthly things.

—THOMAS AQUINAS (1225–74)

CHAPTER 6

To Help Us with the Difficulties of Everyday Life

The angel of the Lord encampeth round about them that fear him, and delivereth them.
—Psalm 34:7

Angel in the Courtroom

IT WAS A CRISP NOVEMBER MORNING in 1995. My husband and I walked to the courthouse for the termination hearing of our two-year old foster son, whom we had had since he was four months old. He was a shaken baby who had suffered severe damage. When we first took him to the doctors, they had said he would be blind and deaf, and that he would never walk or talk. But one month later, while at church, Anthony's eyes and ears opened when he was prayed for. Now two years later he was walking and saying a few words.

As we walked we wondered what would happen, knowing that Anthony's fate was in the hands of the judicial system and the state. The case workers and lawyers said the judge probably would not terminate his right to be taken back by his biological parents. We only hoped they would. In Pennsylvania the courts do not easily give up rights to children when the biological parents are incarcerated. We had raised Tony from a baby, given him our love, and we felt like he was ours. He did not recognize or even know his biological mother.

The hearing got underway. I testified, along with physicians and numerous therapists, but could not tell how things were going. I felt helpless. Nearly an hour had passed and testimony was closing. I prayed silently, concentrating on God, and tried not to be nervous. Suddenly my vision grew foggy and blurry. I thought it was the flourescent lighting, and looked around the room, but nothing changed.

The judge was about to give her decision. As she spoke, her voice started to break, as if to fight off tears, and she grabbed a glass of water to get control of herself. I began blinking, trying to retain focus, and as I looked up, directly behind the judge stood a huge angel with a broad stance. He had a spear in his hand but was at ease. I was flooded with such peace and warmth, it was almost unreal. I knew all was well and everything would be okay.

The judge gained her composure and agreed to terminate. She terminated parental rights, which would give us a chance to adopt. When the judge spoke her verdict, the angel was gone.

Michelle Peters
York, Pennsylvania

HEAVEN'S CONNECTION—THE FREE PHONE CALL

One day while my wife and I were in Capetown, South Africa, I was in a car accident. I wanted to let my daughter, Kelley, back in the States, know about it. When I phoned her, nobody was at home. Thirty minutes later, the phone rang in my hotel room. I picked it up, and Kelley was on the phone. I said, "Kelly, how did you know we were in Capetown."

"I didn't know," she said.

"Well, how did you know I was in this hotel?" I asked.

"I didn't know," she repeated.

I got frustrated and said, "Well, how come you're on this phone then?"

"How are you on this phone?" she echoed.

I said, "I didn't call you."

She said, "I didn't call you either. I just walked in the door and my phone was ringing. When I answered it you were on the other end of the line."

I said, "Hey, that's God!"

And when we left the hotel, the telephone call to America was not listed on the hotel bill.

Rev. Don Ikerd
Kenya, Africa

THE OTHER PERSON'S FOOTPRINTS

Dustin, my California-bred guide dog, was having trouble outside our Long Island apartment. This was his first snowstorm and he was confused. I'm blind, and I wasn't doing so well either. No one was out, so there were no sounds to steer me. Contrary to what many people think, guide dogs do not find the way for a blind person. The blind person directs the dog.

After a harrowing forty-five minutes, Dustin and I finally made it back. But guide dogs must be walked regularly. "Next time why don't you ask God to go with you?" a friend suggested. And so I did. "Lord, go with Dustin and me. The wind is so fierce it's hard to concentrate on our direction. Lead us."

Snow stung our faces and it was difficult to make a path. Dustin whined a little. "Okay, boy," I said to him, "the Lord is with us." And then I gave him a command that a blind person gives only when another person is leading the way: "Dustin, follow!"

Dustin perked up and to my astonishment took off as though he knew exactly where to go. We made it to the street, then headed back to our building—no problem.

A young woman trudged up and offered to walk us to our door. "We'll just follow your footprints," she said. "Yours and the dog's, and that other person's."

"What other person?" I asked.

"There's a dog's prints. And your prints. And a larger person's prints. Wasn't someone with you?"

I paused for a moment and then I answered, "Oh yes, there was Someone with us." There always is.

Sandy Seltzer
Mineola, New York
Guideposts

THE INVISIBLE HAND

My husband, Ray, had not returned from his first hemodialysis at the medical center. It was 7:00 P.M. He knew I had an important meeting at eight and had insisted that I not wait for him.

I grabbed my car keys and left our apartment at 7:30. Taking the hall steps at a fast clip, I was stopped on the second step—physically stopped. An insistent feeling made me go back to the apartment.

After fifteen minutes of pacing, I began to feel foolish. I put on my coat and started down the steps. Again I was stopped. It was as though a hand held me back. I retreated, unlocked the door and reentered the apartment. I sat down in a chair by the telephone and waited.

At eight o'clock I heard fumbling at the door. When I opened it, Ray stood there ashen-faced and shivering. Helping him inside, I wrapped him in a comforter and took his temperature. Ninety degrees! After he'd had some hot soup and coffee, the color began to seep back into his face.

Later I found out what had happened at the center. Apparently, the fluid levels on the machine had been set incorrectly. Too much fluid had been pulled from Ray's body, and he went into shock. He had been treated and released when he said he was okay. But during the forty-minute drive home in a car with a heater that didn't work, he had had a relapse.

"Thank God you were home," he said. "Honey, I prayed you'd be here."

Carol Anderson
Guideposts

THE NAME ON THE MAILBOX

"Be bold and mighty forces will come to your aid." That's an adage I've long believed in. But there was a moment in my life that has led me to believe that if you're bold, sometimes mysterious forces will come to your aid.

At that time, when my family was struggling, I sought a job with Oklahoma's Department of Human Services. This was a bold move, for I had no diploma, having dropped out of school to marry, but eventually I passed a test and got the job.

My assignment was locating and assisting needy families, and locating them was often difficult. This particular day in 1977, I'd heard of a needy family (no father present, little money or food, frightened mother and children) living near Lake Texoma. This was dangerous country, but I felt it was my duty to find them. I drove all morning with little to guide me, and in this gun-crazy backcountry you didn't just knock on any shack and ask for directions.

Finally, in early afternoon I parked in the shade of a cottonwood and began to pray, asking God to direct me. I then looked down the lane I'd already driven over twice, and there was a lone mailbox plainly emblazoned with the family's name.

My visit went well; we'd been able to help this family with food and clothing. As

I was leaving, the grateful mother marveled that I'd found her house. "It wasn't hard," I said, "once I saw your name on the mailbox."

"My name?" the woman said to me obviously mystified.

And going back to the road, I examined the mailbox again. There was no name. No name at all.

Virginia Cottrell
Guideposts

The Lost Key

Our twenty-two-year-old son, Nathaniel lost the key to his truck. After he had searched for it everywhere and hadn't been able to find it, he asked me to help him. I looked and could not find it either, so I asked the other children to help us. We all searched high and low for the one lone key. I personally turned his room upside down looking for it. We even took his bedspread completely off the bed and shook it up and down, but no key could be found.

Finally in desperation, we all gathered in the family room, knelt down and prayed to God to help us find the lost key. After prayer I felt a strong impression to go back into his room and look again, so we did.

When we entered his bedroom, there in plain sight was the key on top of the bedspread we had just shaken. We all looked at one another in wonderment. We knew it had not been on the bed before we prayed, but after asking God for help, He had sent an angel to find the lost key and place it there.

Joy Haney
Stockton, California

Angel in the Fog

My first encounter with an angel was on my way to a special morning prayer meeting which was being held at my church. It was approximately 4:45 A.M. on an unusually foggy day. The visibility was probably zero. My daughter had warned me the night before about the road conditions, and had discouraged me from driving at that time. It was the thickest fog I had ever seen.

Due to the fog, I got lost. I drove around for about forty-five minutes, and did not know where I was. I was so disoriented I began to panic. Rolling down the window, I yelled at the top of my lungs, "Jesus! Help me, I'm lost!"

At the instant those words left my mouth, I heard someone yell back at me, "Hey, you're going the wrong way!" I looked in the direction that I heard the voice and saw a figure that turned out to be a man in a car, in the lane next to me facing the opposite direction. I said pleadingly to him, "Help me. I'm lost!"

He replied back to me, "Where are you going?" I told him I was going to a prayer meeting at the Christian Life Center. He told me to make a U-turn and follow him. I did exactly what he said. Within just a few minutes, we were at the entrance of the church. He then made a welcoming gesture with his hand out of the car window and said, "Here."

I glanced up and was able to make out the "Christian Life Center" marquee. When I looked back at the gentleman who had helped me, he was gone. In the time that it took for me to glance up at the marquee and back again, he had disappeared. I didn't even see red tail lights.

After praying at the church, I went to work. When I arrived at work, I told my co-worker, Mary, about my experience.

"Yoshie!" she said excitedly, "don't you know that was an angel from God, sent to help you?"

"Ooh!" I exclaimed, as a chill came over my body. I was shaking all over for quite a while. I will never forget my first encounter with an angel!

Yoshie H. Brown
Stockton, California

THE LIGHT IN THE BLIZZARD

My daughter Sandi and I were driving home to Tennessee after spending Thanksgiving with relatives in Detroit. As we neared the Cumberland Mountains, we hit a blinding snowstorm. The radio warned of treacherous conditions. Phone lines were down. Ours was the lone car approaching the foothills.

Straightening in her seat, Sandi gripped the steering wheel tightly. "Dad's expecting us," she said. I was anxious to get back too. "Okay," I agreed, "let's keep going."

We started uphill. I strained to see the signs marking the winding road, but the wipers were no match for the driving snow. "I can't see," Sandi said. I'd made a terrible decision. We couldn't turn around. "God, please guide us," we prayed aloud.

"Look!" I shouted. A glowing light shone hazily in the distance, about 50 feet ahead. "Follow that vehicle!" Snow covered even the road signs now, but the light moved on steadily, like a beacon.

An hour passed, and we began our descent. The light slowed until it barely advanced. Through every bend and dip in the road, the distance between us remained constant until finally we rounded the last curve. We looked ahead. Not one other vehicle was on the road.

We wanted to thank our guide. "He's got to be in here," Sandi said, pulling into a diner. When we walked in, the customers stared. "How did you get over the mountain?" the waitress asked. "No one has come across in hours."

The all-powerful Light had guided us.

Muriel S. Hurst
Maryville, Tennessee
Guideposts

The very presence of an angel is a communication. Even when an angel crosses our path in silence, God has said to us, "I am here. I am present in your life."

—TOBIAS PALMER (1926–)

CHAPTER 7

To Help in the Time of Crisis

Bless the Lord, ye his angels, that excel in strength, that do his commandments, hearkening unto the voice of his word.
—PSALM 103:20

THE LITTLE GIRL ANGEL

N OCTOBER 17, 1997, our son-in-law, George Sievers, who pastors in Dublin, Texas, was driving down the freeway south of Dallas in his new truck, accompanied by his seven-year-old daughter, Bethany. Suddenly be blanked out. The truck went across the divider, hit a tree, crashed and fell down a cliff, hitting another tree.

Both George and Bethany were wearing seat belts, and at the time of the crash the airbags were released, but George was knocked unconscious. Bethany remained conscious but confused, especially since her daddy seemed to be asleep. She was feeling very much alone when suddenly an angel appeared—a little girl angel with a glow above her head—and sat right next to Bethany. She spoke to Bethany and said, "Don't be afraid! Everything will be all right."

Eventually George and Bethany were airlifted out of the truck by a helicopter and taken to two different hospitals. The truck was totaled—only the cabin remained intact.

Three hours later Beth, Bethany's mother, walked into the emergency room at children's hospital and found Bethany. Bethany was so excited, all she could talk about was her angel. They released her from the hospital with no scratches or bruises. George was released the same day with nothing wrong with him. It was a miracle neither one was hurt.

Later I asked my granddaughter what happened to the angel, and she said, "She flew out the window."

Theresa DeMerchant
Missionary to Brazil

THE INVISIBLE MERCEDES-BENZ

We were doing missionary work in Kenya, Africa, and decided to visit some friends of ours who lived in war-torn Ethiopia. While we were there with Ethiopian missionary Teklemara, an uprising started.

"We need to get out of this war zone," Teklemara said. The three of us boarded a bus, but it didn't go very far before it ran out of gas. Teklemara tried to flag down cars to pick us up, but no one would stop. My wife and I began to pray that God would send someone to help us. Out of nowhere a big white Mercedes Benz pulled up to where we were standing and stopped. Teklemara asked the driver if he would take us out of the war zone. The driver just nodded his head; he did not say a word.

My wife and I got in the back seat and waved good-bye to Teklemara. As the car began to move, my wife leaned forward to talk to the driver, but when she saw a big machine gun in his lap, she hurriedly leaned back and whispered to me, "I wonder whose side he's on?"

Then we noticed a road block up ahead. I said to her, "I guess we'll know in a minute whose side he's on." When we came to the roadblock, the driver just drove on through.

A little farther on down the road was another roadblock. When we drove through the second roadblock without being stopped, I whispered to my wife, "He's some high official. That's why they're letting him by."

Then we came to a third road block with many soldiers around it. When we drove right through this one, we began to realize that an angel had been sent to deliver us. My wife looked back at the soldiers after we went through this third road block, and they were continuing their conversations as if they hadn't even seen us. God had made us invisible to their eyes!

All the way to Addis Ababa, the driver did not talk. We tried to give him money for helping us, but he just took off and left us standing safely at our destination.

"God didn't send an old Ford or beat up Toyota after us," my wife said. "He sent the very best—a brand new Mercedes Benz."

Rev. Don Ikerd
Kenya, Africa

THE UNCANNY SOS

Vietnam, December 14, 1967—just before the first Tet Offensive. I was with Charlie Company, First Battalion, 25th Lightning Division, near Saigon. In the afternoon, a Vietcong death squad hit us, leaving ten dead. At sundown, feeling jittery, I went on patrol. Gribbit, Vigor and I set up a listening post about five hundred meters from camp. At 1:00 A.M., I reported in: "This is Charlie, L.P. One. Lots of movement out here."

The radio on my back crackled: "Get down...we're going to fire." Our guys started throwing rockets into the bush; the enemy started their own barrage. We were pinned down. "O God! Get us *out* of here...please!" I prayed as I chewed dirt.

There was a thud, like someone punching my back. A grenade exploded. I felt blood trickling down my back. "We've been hit," I radioed, "we're coming in!" In spite of our wounds, we scrambled in the darkness through a field of claymore mines and bales of razor-sharp wire and stumbled into the arms of the arriving medics.

Three weeks later, when all three of us were out of the hospital and back at camp, my platoon sergeant called me in. "Cloverdale, how did you guys manage to let the medics know you'd been hit?"

"Radio, sir." I was surprised she should ask.

"Not with *this*, soldier," he replied, holding up a twisted, blackened box. It was the radio I had carried on my back. It had taken the full blast of the grenade, probably saving my life. And in doing so, the batteries, the crystal— every component—had been destroyed.

How did the medics get my SOS? I don't know. But God does.

Thomas Coverdale
Guideposts

THE INVISIBLE COMPANION

I was driving home after visiting my family for Christmas. Traffic on the two-lane road was slow but steady. A fine mist saturated the cold air, and as the temperature dropped, the highway grew slick.

Suddenly my wheels skidded and the brakes locked. The guardrail was coming up fast! I cried out, "God, help me!" The impact of the crash threw me over the seat and I blacked out.

I woke up on the floor in the backseat. A man and a boy were bent over me. "You hit a patch of ice," the man said. "A policeman saw the whole thing. He's radioing for help."

Peering out the window, I realized that my car had been moved to the opposite side of the highway and parked safely on the grass off the shoulder. *How in the world did I get over here?* Before I could ask, another car hit the same patch of ice and spun into the guardrail—at the exact spot I had. The man and his son ran to help.

When trucks arrive to sand the road, father and son returned with the policeman. "By the way," the policeman said, "what happened to your companion?"

I looked at him quizzically: "What companion?"

"He drove the car to this spot," the officer said. "I saw him."

"We saw him too," said the father. "He crossed the lane of oncoming traffic and parked right here. But no one got out. In fact, we had to break a window to get in."

There had been no man in my car. But Someone had been with me.

Dorothy Howard
Guideposts

PULLED FROM THE FLOOD

My classmate Pam and I had been studying for college midterms at a quiet picnic area outside town when we saw dark clouds gathering. We quickly packed up, stuffed half a semester's notes in a cardboard box on the back of my motorcycle, and got going. We had made it to the edge of Tucson when the storm hit.

The temperature plummeted and the wind howled. Then came hailstones that sounded like machine-gun fire on our helmets. Without warning the heavy traffic slowed in front of us. I braked to a stop, and when I put my boot down to balance the bike, it splashed into water up to my ankle. The six-lane road had become a river. "Get to dry land!" I shouted to Pam.

She jumped off the back of the motorcycle and sloshed her way among the cars to the safety of a nearby restaurant doorway.

As I walked toward her a knee-deep wave toppled the bike and proceeded to drag me down the street under it. Icy water saturated my clothes and filled my helmet. I couldn't push the 500-pound motorcycle off me. Then churning water rushed into my mouth and nose. I realized I could drown! *Lord, this is not how I would have done it,* I thought.

Suddenly I felt someone grab my collar and yank me up out of the water. I found myself looking into the bearded face of a man. He was wearing a dark ski cap and plaid flannel jacket. He was bigger than anyone I had ever seen. He held me suspended in one hand. With the other he reached down and picked up my motorcycle. He dragged me to "shore," where Pam waited, mouth agape. He set me and the bike on the wet sidewalk and looked down at me.

"You okay?" he asked, his quiet voice seeming to float above the storm. I nodded. "Good," he said. He turned and walked over to a Volkswagen and drove away while the other cars were still stalled in the water.

Pam and I went inside the restaurant to settle down, and the owner gave us blankets and hot chocolate. "Our notes!" Pam cried. "Are they still on the back of the bike?"

The owner dashed out and returned a second later with a soggy cardboard box. Pam and I peeled back the lid. Our notes were bone-dry! We took our exams as scheduled and I thanked God for helping me get an *A* on the test. The course, by the way, was a good one: a survey of Christian literature.

Stephen M. Hale
Austin, Texas

OUT OF THE MIRE

A misty rain fell on our construction crew as we climbed a mountain near La Grande, Ore. Our job was to remove rock from a pipeline ditch and put in a gas line. As the swamper, I cleaned mud from the heavy machinery parts and then greased them. I was still working when the other guys decided to break for lunch and take off to a point about 1000 feet down the mountain. "Meet us when you can, Mac," they called out.

By the time I finished, I was soaking wet, muddy and greasy from head to foot. There was no way I could eat my lunch without washing first. I looked into the ditch, which was filled with water. *Easy way to wash up*, I thought. I jumped in, expecting to stand knee-deep in water, but instead I was completely immersed, and to make matters worse my boots were stuck in mud up to my shins.

Frantically I tugged at one leg, then the other, only to be pulled in deeper. Mud had reached my chest and the weight of the water was pressing down. *Oh, God, please help.*

Finally I could hold my breath no longer. I exhaled and felt my body descend. My throat burned as the muddy water rushed inside me. Then I blacked out.

The next thing I knew I was lying face-down on the bank of the ditch, as if I had been dragged to safety. I looked for one of the crew. No one was there. No muddy footprints, no tracks, no evidence of help...except for His.

M. M. McIntosh
Pascagoula, Mississippi

THE OTHER TWO PASSENGERS

Wendy was driving with her friends Hope and Luke. They expected to be gone about a total of twenty minutes, got about a mile-and-a-half from our house and a man in a pick-up truck ran a red light. He hit them broadside at quite a speed. They skidded sideways, rolled over three times, spun around a few times and finally stopped right side up in the middle of the road.

Wendy and Hope were in the front seat with their seat belts on; Luke was in the back without his seatbelt fastened. Hope ended up with only a few minor scratches on one shin, and Luke only had to get five stitches in his head. That's it! No other injuries. But two witnesses, two different Police Officers, said they saw five people in the car: two in front and three in back, and the paramedics kept asking Wendy, Hope and Luke where the other two people were. They kept insisting there were five. I'm sure those other two were angels! Thank the Lord for His protection.

To see the car you would think for sure someone had been killed. It is a miracle that none of the three in the accident had any broken bones. All the windows were completely broken out except one passenger side back window. The front driver's side wheel was totally broken off the axle. At the point of impact on the driver's side, the whole side is pushed all the way to the middle of the car. It's a mess, but the kids are fine!

Karen Bridegroom

And flights of angels sing thee to thy rest!

—WILLIAM SHAKESPEARE (1564–1616)
Hamlet, Act V, Sc. 2

To Soothe Our Fears in the Time of Sickness and Distress

The angels....Are they not all ministering spirits, sent forth to minister for them who shall be heirs of salvation?

—HEBREWS 1:13–14

❧

THE WHITE LIGHT

OUR EIGHT-YEAR-OLD DAUGHTER, AUTUMN, hadn't slept well in days. She was suffering from a bad case of chicken pox, and her fever had spiked to 104. Her skin was covered with itchy red patches that she was trying her best not to scratch.

That night I went to her bedroom. "Honey, I want you to sleep downstairs, so I can hear you if you need me," I said. "Daddy's got the couch all ready."

In the living room I tucked her in, covering her with an afghan. I gently stroked Autumn's head. *God, please comfort her tonight*, I asked as I stifled a yawn.

Exhausted, I went straight to bed myself. As I slid between the cool, smooth sheets and rested my head on the pillow, I realized I had forgotten to put a top sheet over Autumn. *The afghan could aggravate her skin*, I worried, half asleep. *I should get up.* With my toes, I could feel the fresh, clean, folded sheet I had set out at the foot of my bed. *I'll get up and cover her...*

My eyes opened with the sunrise next morning. Autumn! How could I have fallen asleep before making absolutely sure she was comfortable? I rushed into the living room, feeling awful.

Leaning over my sleeping girl, I pressed my cheek to her forehead. Her fever had broken! As I pulled the afghan away from her face, a piece of white sheet peeked out from underneath. Relieved, I went to make breakfast.

"I'm glad you covered Autumn with the sheet after I went to bed," I told my husband when he came into the kitchen.

"I didn't," he said. "I went to bed right after you. You were out like a light."

"But Autumn couldn't have done it herself..."

Just then she dashed in, bright-eyed. "Hi, sweetie," I said. "Did you sleep well?"

She nodded. "At first I was uncomfortable. But then something funny happened." Autumn looked at her father, then back at me. "A white light filled one corner of the living room. I wanted to get up and touch it but I was too tired. Then my skin felt cool—not itchy—and I fell asleep!" Autumn grabbed a piece of toast from the table. "Do you think an angel came to tuck me in?"

Susan Grezel
Rockville, Connecticut
Guideposts

THE FOURTH MAN

On Tuesday, May 6, 1997, I woke up at 4:30 A.M. in Mercy General Hospital in Sacramento, California, facing the most dangerous physical experience of my life. At 7:00 A.M. I was scheduled to have open-heart surgery to bypass four blocked arteries in my heart. God had been so good to me for the past four years since I had had my first heart attack. Four years ago the cardiologist had refused to do any invasive treatment to find the extent of my heart attack. This time the cardiologist immediately ordered an angiogram and found the four blocked arteries that had been my problem four years ago. He scheduled heart surgery for the very next day.

At 5:30 A.M. on Tuesday, my wife, Carol, and our dear friend, June Langford, walked into my room to visit and pray with me before surgery. In the next few minutes some men from the church came to pray for me: Ted Graves, Harry Meeks and Richard Ikerd. I didn't recognize the other gentleman. We visited and prayed together, and I told them, "I have absolutely no fear regarding this heart surgery this morning."

The surgery started on schedule at 7:00 A.M. A little over four hours later the surgeon came to the waiting room and told Carol and our friends that I had come through the surgery very well, and there was no heart muscle damage, which surprised him. They all rejoiced in the Lord over the good news.

I progressed through recovery rapidly. The nurses in ICU liked me so well they wouldn't release me to a regular room for two days. To our surprise and thankfulness to God, I was released to go home from the hospital on Saturday, the fifth day after surgery.

All during this time we had visits from friends and family and much prayer. Carol kept a journal of the daily visits and events. During the next week I would periodically ask Carol who had come to pray for me before surgery on Tuesday morning. She would tell me about the three men and June. I knew she was forgetting someone. Finally on Thursday, ten days after surgery she read to me from her journal everyone who visited, called and sent cards.

Friday, May 16, we sat down to eat a delicious dinner a friend, Dawn Karr, had brought to us. Just after we prayed the Lord seemed to open my understanding about the fourth man in the room. It was clear to me all of a sudden that the fourth man in the room was an angel and was only seen by me. I started to choke up with tears. Carol looked at me, jumped up from her chair, rushed over to me and said, "Honey, what is wrong?"

"There was a fourth man in the room," I said.

"What room?" Carold said.

"The hospital room before I went into surgery."

"Where was he standing?" she asked. "Right between June and Ted Graves," I told her.

"What did he look like?"

"He had medium brown hair and was dressed in a white shirt, tie, and light dress pants."

Carol continued to probe. "Did he say anything?" "No," I said, "but he looked at me with eyes full of tenderness and compassion and he had the biggest warm smile on his face."

Carol kept questioning me. "What did he do when we prayed?"

"He prayed with us," I replied.

"When did he leave the room?" she asked.

"He left when the other men left," I told her.

Carol was in tears. She said, "Honey, that was an angel from God! Now, I know why you told us that you had absolutely no fear about your surgery. You felt encouraged and strengthened from this angel God sent you! This is just like the Hebrew children in the fiery furnace. The fourth man was like unto the Son of God!" By this time we both were crying and rejoicing in the Lord.

After my revelation about my angel, Carol read a book entitled, *A Rustle of Angels*. The author, Marilyn Webber, made this statement: "Angel-visited people have described the eyes of these spirits more than any other feature. They were struck by the depth of love and compassion in the angels' eyes, which left them with a deep sense of peace."

I praise God for this special heavenly visitor. His eyes were full of tenderness and compassion which took away all my fear. Facing life-and-death issues and surviving makes life a lot sweeter.

Rev. Harold E. Clemons
Stockton, California

THE SOFT HAND

The years 1995 and 1996 were very stressful for me. At one point I had an eight-day asthma attack. During that time I was put in a nursing home because I could not care for myself. Then a tumor was found in my neck and the doctor put me through all kinds of tests trying to find out how serious and what kind of tumor it was. Because it was cancerous I had to have radiation treatments.

When the doctor came to visit me one day he told me I had to have twenty treatments. The nurse overheard that statement. After the doctor left she told me "If you take twenty treatments on your throat, you will never talk again."

A further blow came when I received the news that my mother was very ill and was not going to live.

During this stressful time, I and my family made the decision to sell the house that my deceased husband and I had lived in for many years. So I put my house up for sale and started looking for a smaller place to live. All the while I was having the scheduled radiation treatments, and was feeling more and more sick.

In February 1996 my mother died. I felt so troubled about everything that it was hard for me to sleep. I would lie awake at night thinking, "Lord, am I doing the right thing by selling my house? Maybe I should cancel the listing." I was so distraught, upset, sick and worried with everything that had happened: the death of my mother, the radiation treatments, the trauma of leaving a home that I had fixed up. It seemed everything in my world was changing and it left me feeling very fearful.

One night when I couldn't sleep, I felt a hand press against my cheek, touching me so tenderly. It felt so good. I thought it was an angel, for I had never felt anything so soft and peaceful. Immediately, I fell asleep and slept all night long. Never again have I had that awful doubt and fear that tormented me in that night.

By the way, I only had fifteen of the scheduled radiation treatments instead of the twenty. It is now February 1998, and I can talk. Every day I praise God for His blessings to me, and I will never forget the night He sent His angel to put me to sleep.

Mildred Watts
Stockton, California

THE ROOM FULL OF ANGELS

In May, 1996, I was diagnosed with melanoma cancer that had been discovered in a birthmark on my leg. When the doctors scheduled my surgery, I called a ladies prayer group that prays *live* on the air once a week, and asked them to pray for me.

They did. They asked the Lord to send His angels into the operating room to be with me. The day of the surgery arrived and the anesthetist came to give me a spinal and to put a light sedation in my IV drip. Towards the end of the surgery, when I was coming out of sedation, I saw that the room was full of people. They were filled with light, dazzling in their brightness, and I felt such a warmth and peace that everything was fine.

I asked the anesthetist who was standing at my head, "Who are all of these people in here?"

"There are only four of us," she said.

I knew then that God had sent His angels to be with me.

Kay LaCoss
Stockton, California

NURSE WITH A SMILE

When my husband, Johnny, entered a hospital in Houston, Texas, two large aneurysms pressed on his heart and spinal cord. Johnny was scared and uncertain. The surgery might leave him paralyzed and he didn't want to live as an invalid. We prayed for God's guidance in this decision. Finally Johnny asked me to leave for a while so he could think.

I went to get a cup of coffee with my brother Jack, who had come with us. "Without that operation," I told him, "Johnny probably won't live out the year."

When Jack and I returned an hour later Johnny was alone in his room, smiling. "You have to meet my nurse, Shu-Lin," he said. "She has convinced me to have the operation."

Shu-Lin had assured Johnny he was in good hands, and promised to pray for him. "Not to worry," she had said. How had she given my husband confidence when the doctors and I couldn't? "You'll understand when you see her smile," Johnny said.

Jack and I met Shu-Lin later that afternoon. She was everything Johnny had described—Asian in appearance, warm, caring and cheerful, with a brilliant smile.

My sister Jane arrived to be with us for the surgery, and we went to the waiting room. Shu-Lin accompanied Johnny into surgery. It was her day off, but she said she wanted to be there. During the operation, she returned periodically to let us know how Johnny was doing. Each time she appeared, we felt relief and optimism. Finally the surgery was over, and Shu-Lin came to give us the good news even before the doctor reported to us.

Johnny spent the next five days in intensive care. Often he woke up to find Shu-Lin wiping his forehead or holding his hand. When he was out of danger, Shu-Lin came to say good-bye. "I must go now," she said. "Others need me."

The following week, Johnny was well enough to go home. We decided I should find Shu-Lin to thank her for being so kind. But when I inquired about her, the nurses on duty just looked at me: They had never heard of her. Johnny and Jack and Jane and I *knew* she had been with us. I went to the administration office, determined to locate Shu-Lin. But I was told there was no such employee.

At that moment I realized: Hospitals don't keep records of guardian angels.

Sue Bryson
Roswell, Georgia
Guideposts

❧

It is in rugged crises, in unweariable endurance, and in aims which put sympathy out of the question, that the angel is shown.

—Ralph Waldo Emerson (1803–82)

To Help When We Pray Heartfelt Prayers

For he shall give his angels charge over thee, to keep thee in all thy ways.
—PSALM 91:11

∾

THE MYSTERIOUS MAGAZINE

HILE I WAS A PASTOR in Arizona, God started talking to me about going to Kenya, Africa, as a missionary. One night I had a dream about a missionary who was already there. In the dream the Lord told me that he wanted me to go. Several weeks later that missionary was killed. Then I knew God had spoken to me.

Just to make sure, at 8:00 one morning, while I was praying, I said, "God, I'm going to put you on a two-hour test. I want you to send me in the mail a magazine with an article about Kenya in it." Ten minutes before 10:00 A.M., the mail was delivered, including a magazine wrapped up in brown paper. There on the cover were these words: "Revival in East Kenya, Africa." God did not send just one little article; he sent a magazine full of articles about Kenya.

"Where did this magazine come from?" I wondered. I looked at the address and found out that it had come to the wrong address. God sent an angel to reroute that magazine right to my doorstep just in time.

Rev. Don Ikerd
Africa

THE FANTASTIC REUNION

My family history is a little crazy. My father has been married three times and my mother at least five. When my mother and father married, she already had three children, and then they had two more. I was one of the two. When I was about three years old, my mother left all five children and we were separated. We children went to live with our own father. My father remarried when I was seven. As a result I never knew about one of my brothers.

In 1993, I became heavily burdened and could not understand why. That year I found out that I had an older brother named Gregory Underwood. By that time I had been reunited with all my other siblings, with that one exception. Gregory was born in the 50s and was half-black. Because that was totally unacceptable at the time, he had been sent away to live in Sacramento. When I found out that he had joined the navy, I asked the navy to try and locate him. My letter was returned—they had no information about him.

I began to pray for him. I also asked that God would let our paths cross one day so I could witness to him about God and let him know that he was loved, despite his rejection. Then I decided to go to the Department of Motor Vehicles. They provide a service in which you fill out a form and they will contact the person for you. They will notify you if the person is located, but it is that person's option whether they will contact you or not. On the day that I went to DMV to fill out the form, I had to go to the credit union. We bank at a small credit union on Broadway so I am familiar with all the tellers. That day I noticed a new face. The woman who is normally on duty was not there. The new woman was a black woman with the most beautiful smile. She asked me how my day was, and I excitedly explained that I was trying to locate my brother. She knew a lot of people, she said, and wanted to know my brother's name.

"Surely it's not possible for you to know him," I said. "We were separated as children, and I have no way of knowing where he might be."

"Try me," she said.

"Gregory Underwood."

At that she grabbed my hand and asked, "What is his mother's name?" I told her and she asked, "His father's name?" I told her, and her eyes brightened. "Honey," she said, "I know your brother! I have a friend in Sacramento who dated your brother for eight years. He is now a police officer in Seattle, Washington."

I could not believe this! How could this be?

Somehow she gave my phone number to his family and he called. I never saw the woman again. I believe God sent an Angel! After thirty-two years I finally met my brother. He's still in very much pain, but he knows that I love him and that God loves him.

Cindi Friedli
Stockton, California

THE FLYING VAN

In early 1982, while working in El Salvador as a missionary, my wife and I decided to go visit our missionary friend Wynn T. Drost, who was then working in Guatemala. He and his family had formerly been missionaries to El Salvador.

This was during the war in El Salvador when over eighty thousand people lost their lives. The terrorists had a way of stopping the vehicles during the war.

They would put large tree trunks or rocks across the roads, often on curves that were on upgrades in the mountains, so that motorists could not go around the blocks, but would be forced to stop.

At the time of our trip from El Salvador to Guatemala, we drove a Toyota Hiace, a four-cylinder van that sat fairly low on the ground. While driving up one side of a mountain, we made a sharp turn and the lights of the van outlined large boulders that the guerrillas had placed across the road to ambush us. We could not go to the right because the road had been cut out of the side of the mountain. We could not go to the left, because there was a several hundred-foot drop off. At that moment, the men who were hidden in the bushes were undoubtedly ready to come out and see what they would do to us. All we could do was call on Jesus. As we called out the name of Jesus, we felt the power of God begin to work. We did not see angels, but they were around our car.

Suddenly the van was lifted up and it seemed as though we flew over the rocks. Then the angels set us down on the other side—and we continued to travel on our way!

Our van never touched the boulders in the road, and we were never stopped. The terrorists, I'm sure, were amazed at the flying van that night in 1982!

Bruce Howell
Missionary to San Salvador, El Salvador

TAUGHT BY AN ANGEL

Ella Lee Kilgore was born into a family without a father. He had been killed six weeks before she was born. Her mother worked hard twelve-hour days in the fields. As Ella Lee grew older she could not go to school because of the work load in helping with the other children. Her mother would teach the children a few basic words to read, but they were not very literate.

So Ella Lee grew up without knowing how to read much. One day she prayed, "O Lord God, I want to read your Word!" One day while she had the Bible in her hands and was trying to read it, a miracle happened! An invisible angel came and when she did not know how to pronounce a word, the angel would pronounce it for her. From that day forward, whenever she would get the Bible out to read, she would hear the sweetest voice of the angel reading a passage verse by verse. Tears would stream down her face during those precious moments.

She could not read anything else; she could only read the Bible, for I would have to read any letters or important papers that came to her.

Ima Jean Kilgore
Houston, Texas

THE SHACKLES FELL OFF

My son Erick, who was incarcerated at the St. Louis Jail in Missouri, knew he was going to be transferred to Illinois. He had a great fear of the shackles he knew were going to be put on his feet. He prayed, "God, I'm so afraid. Please, help me! Give me a sign showing that you are with me."

When the time arrived for the transfer, leg shackles were put on all the prisoners. When Erick got on the bus, suddenly his shackles fell off. The guards immediately noticed it and asked him if he had a wooden leg. Then they asked his friend if Erick had a key to open the lock that had him bound. When they found out he had no key and no wooden leg, they scratched their heads in puzzlement.

When Erick was going to be transferred the second time to Oklahoma City, I prayed, "O God, when they transfer him again, let the shackles fall off a second time, so he will not discount the first miracle." Sure enough, when he got on the bus, the shackles fell off the second time. Again the guards were dumbfounded, while Erick grinned from ear to ear. Surely God was with him even in the prison. Erick felt like the falling off of the shackles was a sign that he was delivered from drugs, for he does not crave them anymore.

Betty Whayne
St. Louis, Missouri

THE EASTERN AIRLINES EMPLOYEE

It had been a long, tiresome day as my wife and I began walking up the west concourse of the St. Louis airport. I noted the time, 11:22 P.M. The plane had parked at the extreme west end of the concourse. It could not have parked any further away from the luggage carousel.

Upon reaching the baggage carousel, we waited about fifteen minutes for our luggage to arrive. Getting it all together, we started walking toward a taxi stand when my wife turned to me and asked, "Fred, where's your briefcase?"

"Oh, no!" I answered, "I've left it back in the plane. I set it down by my seat next to the window. Our tickets are in it and things I need for tomorrow's board meetings. I've got to go get it!"

Pulling all the luggage back near a seat, I told my wife to wait for me as I went back to the plane, hoping the ramp door would not yet be locked.

As I walked back that long concourse it seemed my feet weighed a ton. By the time I got back to the ramp door, it was closed and locked. I asked people in the area if they knew where the man was who had locked the door. No one had seen him. The only thing I thought to do was go back to the baggage area and see if I could find someone there. So I started on that long walk again—which this time seemed twice as long. It was now 12:15 A.M. Arriving back at the baggage carousel, I found no one around. The place looked deserted.

I was so tired after three trips up and down the concourse that I sat down to rest for a moment. As I sat there a porter came by to help someone else who had arrived on the same plane as we did. I got to him right away.

He told me where to find the luggage claim area for Eastern Airlines. I went but could find no one there. I reported back to the porter and he said as soon as he took care of his customer, he'd see what he could do.

Shortly thereafter, he came and said we'd go back to the plane. For the fourth time I started walking that long trip to the far end of the concourse. Upon arriving he discovered the ramp door locked and he could find no one in the vicinity that had a key. He stopped at a phone and tried to call the baggage claim area, but no one answered there.

When he got no answer, I asked, "What will I do now?"

"The only thing I can tell you is to go back to the baggage area and wait until someone arrives at the claim office. I just hope they haven't gone home," he answered.

He left, and I faced that long concourse for the fifth time. I was about two-thirds of the way back when I remembered that probably the best thing I could do was to pray.

I looked up and down that deserted concourse and not one person was in sight. As I went dragging along, I closed my eyes and prayed desperately, "God, you know the predicament that we're in. Please, put me in touch with the right man to take care of this problem of ours!" It couldn't have taken over ten seconds to pray that prayer.

When I opened my eyes, to my amazement, walking to my left about a step in front of me was a man with an Eastern Airlines emblem on his coat sleeve. Taking a quick step, I touched his shoulder. As he turned, I asked, "Are you an Eastern employee?"

"Yes," he answered, "Why?"

I told him we had just arrived an hour ago on a plane from Atlanta and I had left my briefcase on it. It was very important that I have it as my plane tickets and other needed materials were in it.

"Why, I went through that plane not over a half-hour ago and I didn't see any briefcase. Are you sure you left it on the plane?" he questioned me.

"Yes," I answered, "I know I left it on the plane. You'd never see it if you weren't looking for it. It was leaning against the side of the plane next to the window in aisle twenty-one."

"Well, come on and we'll go back and see," he said.

So for the sixth time I started down that longer-than-ever concourse, but this time with high hopes in my heart and a great big "Thank you, Jesus" on my lips!

When my wife saw me coming with the briefcase, she gave a great big sigh of relief. I'll never know where the man came from. But there's one thing I'm sure of: God had him step out beside me at the precise moment that I prayed for help.

Rev. Fred Kinzie
Toledo, Ohio

The angels—happening that way
This dusty heart espied—
Tenderly took it up from toil
And carried it to God—

—EMILY DICKINSON (1830–86)

To Encourage Us

...behold, angels came and ministered unto him.
—MATTHEW 4:11

~

TWO EXTRA PLACE SETTINGS

N THE SPRING OF 1986, my husband and I returned to the United States from Germany, expecting to return to missionary work in a few months. Instead, we found ourselves pastoring a church in Benton, Arkansas. This was a very low time in my life. I didn't know anyone in Benton and felt all alone. We had expected to be back in Germany or at least with familiar friends and family in Indiana.

Just a few days after moving to Arkansas, a woman named Margaret Hardin called me and asked if I was going to go to a ladies' conference in Arkansas she was attending. I hadn't planned on going as I didn't know my way around the state and wasn't close enough to anyone to travel with them. Margaret then invited me to go with her to the conference. All I had to do was get to her church.

After we arrived at the conference, we discovered that the headquarters hotel where she was staying, was full. There was no room for me there, so she took me across the road to a small hotel where, once again, I was alone.

At this point I was feeling very lonely and friendless. I called my husband to cry on his shoulder. He listened for a few minutes, then asked a very pointed question, "Are you going to have a good time, or sit in your room and cry?" Looking back now, I see that the question came from the Lord, but at the time I felt that no one cared.

I got dressed and was ready when Margaret Hardin picked me up. The service was good and an official's wife asked if I would speak the next morning in the Foreign Missions service. Needless to say, I felt an overwhelming sense of responsibility. When I was dropped off at my hotel, the same feelings of loneliness and hopelessness returned. I took my Bible and lying down across the bed, whispered to the Lord that I didn't have a thing to say that would encourage these women.

Immediately, a Presence entered my room. This Presence lingered all night long. I don't remember praying, but the Lord ministered to my spirit. I didn't sleep that night, and in the morning I felt so wonderful that I walked across to the Waffle House to get some coffee before being picked up for the meeting. I took my Bible and notebook, knowing that I would now be able to write something for the service.

The waitress seated me and set the table for three places. I noticed but didn't pay too much attention, as I was still feeling the Presence of the Lord. The waitress asked me a very strange question. "Where are the gentlemen?" I stated that I was alone. She looked somewhat puzzled but walked away. Shortly, the waitress returned and said, "When you walked in, there were two men with you. They were leaning down talking with you. I saw them sit down with you— where did they go?"

I still had not comprehended what was happening, so told her once again that no one else was with me. "Okay," she said, and walked away, still leaving the extra silverware and water.

I suddenly realized that God was still with me! The Presence that I had felt, had been seen by this waitress as a confirmation to me that *I am not alone!* God had sent ministering spirits when I was at one of the loneliest times of my life. What seemed to me as one lonely time after another, was just a place where God could minister to me without the distraction of others.

Brenda Cox
Warsaw, Indiana

TWELVE ANGELS

It was a regular night in the Graham's household. My wife was attending a party at one of our friend's home and I was at home with our sons. After a bout of playing with them, wrestling and telling bedtime stories, it was too much to handle. I fell asleep in their room. My wife arrived home and didn't bother to wake me. She went to our room to sleep.

In the night I rose up on my elbow to look at the clock. It read 2:30. As I turned to lie back down, I glanced at the door and a man was looking into our room. In my shock I gruffly said, "Hello!" As the man walked into the room, I saw that he was very large, very tall, dressed completely in white. In my spirit I knew instantly he was an angel. He had sparse blond hair and was on the portly side.

No words were exchanged when he walked in, but the words that came from me were in the form of a request. "God, I want to see your protection over my family." I wondered at myself for asking. Little did I know that the answer would come.

After the words came out of my mouth, into the room walked twelve angels.

Four stood on the right side of the bed, four in front of me at the foot, and four on the left side. Now these angels were not the beautiful pictures of artist's renditions that one normally sees. These were plain-looking people that you might meet on the street. The only difference was their size. They were all floor-to-ceiling height, with large bodies, dressed completely in white cloth (not a silky material) that draped from their shoulders and under their arms. There were both men and women. Two of their faces will be indelibly imprinted in my mind forever.

After they walked into the room I really can't say I was afraid, because I could feel the presence of the Lord. The next words I spoke were, "God, I want to see your protection over my wife." When I said these words, it was as if I was in the Spirit looking down on my wife asleep in our room. There were twelve angels around her in the same formation as in the boy's room.

The only way I can think to describe this experience is to say that if peace were thick maple syrup, I felt as though it had been poured from the top of my head to the bottom of my feet. It felt as if my soul was sleeping on a pillow of pure joy, and I slowly went back to sleep.

The next morning I told my wife of this vision. And I began to tell it at work. That night when I got home my wife asked me to question our oldest son, who is four, to see if he had seen anything. I hadn't said anything to him because I'm gone before he wakes.

"Austin," I asked, "Did you see anything last night after you went to bed?"

"Yeah, Dad," he answered, "Jesus walked into our room last night. It was an angel and his friends."

Wanting to test his answer, I asked, "Austin, were they big or little?"

His answer: "Daddy, they were *thick!*"

How many times has God spared our lives at just the right time or how many spiritual battles have been won because of the protection he has given us? I was reminded of the time Satan came before God and proclaimed he couldn't touch Job because of the "Hedge" God had put around him (Job 1:10). The Lord showed to me his hedge of protection around my family. I want to thank God for allowing me to see His love over my family's lives.

Rev. Randy Graham
Stockton, California

THE BRIGHT LIGHT

Something special occurred during the time I was battling cancer. On January 18, 1972, I woke up at 3:00 in the morning and went out into the family room to pray and read my Bible. About 4:30, my husband joined me. We were so desperate that we had both been fasting and praying for a miracle, and my husband had become extremely weak.

About 5:45, the door bell rang, so my husband went to the door. Because it was dark, he asked, "Who's there?" No one answered, so again he asked, "Who's there?" Again no one answered, but the bell kept ringing incessantly, so he opened the door to see who was there. As he opened the door, a Divine presence came through the door. It filled his body with such strength that he was filled with awe and amazement.

He came back into the family room and said, "Something strange just happened to me. A divine presence came through the door and filled my body with strength." We both sat there in holy awe, for we could feel that same presence filling the whole house.

Our little girl was awakened by the doorbell and she came into the family room also to see who was there. As we three were sitting together in holy awe, we heard a noise in the kitchen, so I got up to go see what it was. As I started to leave the family room, suddenly a great, brilliant light filled the house. I stopped dead in my tracks. I was speechless as tears started to stream down my cheeks. Finally I said, "Honey that was the glory of God." My husband and I both felt strength enter our bodies.

At 8:30, the door bell rang again. Julie, our daughter, went to the door and there stood two little girls who lived across the street. They said breathlessly, "Julie, we just had to come over and ask you. Did you see the light that hung over your house this morning? We were watching out our bedroom window and there was a light that came and hung over your house. It just stayed there. It didn't come over anybody else's house."

Margaret McDonald

THE IMMENSE ANGEL

In 1980, my wife and I were attending theological college to better prepare ourselves for God's work. One Saturday night, I had a very vivid dream. In this dream, a college friend and I were driving down a country road with corn fields on either side of the road. I was driving his car and we were having a good time talking and laughing. The night sky was clear and the moon was shining bright.

In my dream I looked out the passenger side of the car, and suddenly out of nowhere came an angel. He was so immense, it seemed as though his head touched the sky and filled the entire field. I stopped the car and got out to take a closer look.

"What are you doing?" my friend kept asking.

"Look at the angel!" I told him. "Can't you see the angel? It's as big as the sky!"

I fell to my knees and began to weep and worship God. As I worshiped, my friend kept saying, "What angel? I don't see any angel." The more he said that, the more my friend began to fade off the scene, until I was all alone on my knees in the middle of the road with this majestic angel.

At that instant, I woke out of sleep, overjoyed and in awe. I did not sleep the rest of the night.

The next morning I called my pastor, Rev. Dumaresq, and told him about my dream. He said, "Ed, God wants you to know that in your work for him, there will be times when all your friends and family will not be able or available to help you or support you. You are going to feel all alone. But God has assigned an angel to you to stay with you. When those times come, remember the angel of the Lord is with you."

That was seventeen years ago. Since then my wife and I have been through some rough and lonely times. The Lord always brings back that dream and I know my angel is with me to watch over me, to encourage and see me through the lonely times.

Rev. Ed Snyder
Stockton, California

THE RUSH OF PEACE

Have you ever cried, "I can't go on. I can't make it?" As a teenager, I suffered off and on with physical problems that caused me deep emotional problems for several years. Most people did not know this, for being a minister's daughter I had learned to cover my pain well. One particular night, January 8, 1998, when I was alone, I cried to God, "I can't bear it any longer. Please heal me! Please, help me!"

I will never forget what happened. Nothing like it had happened to me before. I had heard much about angels and supernatural occurrences, but it always happened to other people. Until this night, I had never encountered such things.

I was all alone in the house and had lain down to go to sleep. I felt a heaviness and turmoil in my mind and soul. I knew I needed to sleep, but I was so restless that I began to cry. Then I started quoting softly, "The Lord is my shepherd; I shall not want."

Suddenly such a feeling of peace came over me, and I felt a heated pressure in the palms of my hands. It felt like I was floating. I must have dozed off to sleep, for I awakened to an audible voice saying, "I am with you." I sat up with a jerk and thought my Mom or Dad had come into my room, but no one was there. I knew then that God was with me. It was like God put a new heart in me and sent me a breath of fresh air into my lungs. I slept like a baby that night. When I awoke the next morning I felt anew. That was the most peaceful night of my life.

When I was at the end of my rope, the Lord sent a messenger of peace. My life has totally changed since that night. God has healed me of my physical problem. Each day everything gets better and better. I will never forget the warm pressure on my hands and the heat that was transferred into them. Neither will I forget the audible voice that spoke to me when there was no one around. That is no one but God.

Angela Haney
Stockton, California

STRANGER AT THE SPRING

Many people take water for granted. You turn on the tap and out it comes. But my wife, Robbie, and I remember the days when water was not so easy to come by.

During the Depression, Robbie and I and our two young daughters lived in a two-room house close to Robbie's father's farm in Daysville, Tennessee. I worked doing construction on a new road, and I was glad to have the job—even if it meant walking five miles each way.

We had a big wood stove to cook on and keep us warm. But we didn't have electricity or running water. We washed with water from a nearby creek. But we had to carry drinking water all the way from a spring in the pasture. That meant walking some 300 yards up a hill and through a gate, filling a couple of two-and-a-half-gallon buckets, and trudging back to the house again. It tired us all out, especially Robbie, who usually had the girls in tow. Still, we were thankful to God for what we had, and somehow sensed that he knew what we were going through and was in it with us.

One warm Saturday, Robbie took the girls to visit her parents, and I stayed home working in the vegetable garden. I was hoeing away, trying to get over feeling tired and discouraged, when something made me stop and look up. A man was standing in the front yard. He was tall and wore black trousers and the whitest shirt I had ever seen. Our house was isolated, and I always knew if anyone was coming, so I was surprised. "Good morning," the man said in a deep, pleasant voice. "I'm very thirsty. Could you give me a drink of water?"

Any drinking water taken from the buckets in our house meant we would soon have to climb up to the spring again, and even the thought seemed exhausting. But then it occurred to me that this stranger might be pretty exhausted himself. "Sure can," I said, shoving aside my own weariness. "Want something to eat too?"

"Just water," he said.

By now our water supply had been sitting for a while, and I suddenly thought of how much a tired and thirsty man would like a drink of fresh, cool water right from the spring. "You sit down and rest," I said, taking a bucket. "I'm going to get some fresh water for you."

I climbed the hill, came back, and poured the stranger a tall, sprakling glass. He drank it right down. "Wonderful water," he said. "Too bad you have to go so far to get it."

"It would be nice if the spring were closer," I said. "But we have many other blessings."

The stranger smiled, said thanks, and walked off down the road into Daysville. I stood staring after him, feeling good—and a little peculiar. Where had the man come from? Where was he going? I had felt so peaceful in his presence I hadn't even asked.

But I couldn't get him out of my mind. I decided to go into town. Daysville was so small that a stranger would be noticed by everyone, and I would be able to learn more about him. But my friends on the porch at the general store said I was the only one who had come down the road. "We couldn't have missed him," they said.

A few days later there was a downpour. About 30 feet from the house, water began seeping out of the ground. When the rain was over and the earth dried, the trickle was still there. I took my shovel and dug in. Water bubbled out, fresh and fit to drink. It was a new spring—right at the spot where I had first seen the mysterious stranger.

We never had to make that climb up to the pasture again. Our new spring didn't go dry for the next two years we lived there. After we finally moved, there was another downpour, and the spring vanished.

Years have passed since then; today water flows right into our house. And yet I'll never forget that long-ago source of refreshment and peace. The Bible says, "If you have done it to the least of these, you have done it unto me." Well, I guess we did. And got a wellspring in return.

Tom Douglas
Rockwood, Tennessee
Guideposts

Angels and ministers of grace defend us!

—WILLIAM SHAKESPEARE (1564–1616)
Hamlet, Act I, Sc. 4.

Speak Messages from God

The chariots of God are twenty thousand, even thousands of angels; the Lord is among them, as in Sinai, in the holy place.

—Psalm 68:17

OD'S ANGELS ARE A PART of the heavenly kingdom. They are powerful, innumerable, and speak messages from God. In 2 Thessalonians we read that God will "give relief to you who are troubled, and to us as well. This will happen when the Lord Jesus is revealed from heaven in blazing fire with his powerful angels" (1:7, NIV). There are angels who bring messages, angels with swords in their hands, angels who protect, angels who minister. Hebrews tells us "[God] makes his angels spirits....Are they not all ministering spirits, sent forth to minister for them who shall be heirs of salvation?" (1:7–14).

Angels surround the throne of God, and He sends them forth to help, deliver, and strengthen his people. The Book of Revelation shows their position in heaven: "And I beheld, and I heard the voice of many angels round about the throne and the beasts and the elders: and the number of them was ten thousand times ten thousand, and thousands of thousands; saying with a loud voice, Worthy is the Lamb that was slain to receive power, and riches, and wisdom, and strength, and honour, and glory, and blessing" (5:11–12).

Angels are not ghosts.

Angels are created beings who are messengers of God. They are not the ghosts of people who have died. Angels give aid, or bring messages of hope. They do not wander, earthbound, like a lonely spirit. They have a purpose, a mission. Angels sent from God leave you with a calm serenity.

One lady who had felt the touch of an angel during a very stressful time in her life said that she felt a wave of inexpressible sweetness, the sense that everything would be all right.

The message of an angel on a mission of good will is always "Fear not!" Angels are sent to let you know that things are going to work out all right if you follow God's voice, and that He is with you.

The *Oxford Universal Dictionary* gives the following definition of an angel: "A ministering spirit or divine messenger; one of an order of spiritual beings superior to man in power and intelligence, who are the attendants and messengers of Deity."

Angels are exceedingly numerous.

The Scriptures indicate that there are a vast number of angels.

- Jesus told his disciples, "Do you think I cannot call on my Father, and he will at once put at my disposal more than twelve legions of angels?" (Matthew 26:53, NIV).

- "You have come to Mount Zion, to the heavenly Jerusalem, the city of the living God. You have come to thousands upon thousands of angels in joyful assembly" (Hebrews 12:22, NIV).

- "Then I looked and heard the voice of many angels, numbering thousands upon thousands, and ten thousand times ten thousand" (Revelation 5:11, NIV).

- "The chariots of God are twenty thousand, even thousands of angels: the Lord is among them, as in Sinai, in the holy place" (Psalm 68:17).

Angels are powerful.

Daniel experienced an angel's power. He told King Darius, "My God sent his angels, and he shut the mouths of the lions. They have not hurt me" (Daniel 6:22). The strength of *one* angel was more powerful than a den of hungry lions ready to devour him.

Paul describes the ability of angels in 2 Thessalonians 1:7 with the vivid adjective "mighty" (KJV) or "powerful" (NIV) from the Greek word *dunamis*, which is the root of the English word *dynamite*. In terms of their power, God's angels have a force resembling his mighty explosive.

How many firefighters, carrying the most sophisticated equipment, would be needed to save three Hebrew children from a blazing furnace of fire, which had just killed the men that had thrown them into the flames? God sent just one (Daniel 3:25). God sent one angel to help Hezekiah when a huge army surrounded Jerusalem. One angel killed 185,000 men (2 Kings 19:35).

At times they shine with great light.

The angel who rolled away the stone from the tomb of Jesus was not only dressed in white, but shone as brilliant lightning (Matthew 28:3), so much so that the keepers of the tomb shook and became like dead men. Although the stone was too heavy for one man to move, it proved to be a simple task for the angel to move.

Daniel describes the angel he saw in this way: "I looked up and there before me was a man dressed in linen, with a belt of finest gold around his waist. His body was like chrysolite, his face like lightning, his eyes like flaming torches, his arms and legs like the gleam of burnished bronze, and his voice like the sound of a multitude" (Daniel 10:5–6, NIV).

In our time, some who have seen angels speak in awe of the whiteness of their being, or their brilliant colors.

Although they are invisible beings, at times they can be seen.

The king of Syria had dispatched his army to Dothan, because he had learned that the prophet Elisha was there. When Elisha's servant went out for his walk the next morning, he saw the chariots and troops and ran back into the house crying out in fear that they were surrounded. Elisha took the news calmly and told him not to be afraid. There were more troops on his side than there were in the army of the Syrian king, even though the servant couldn't see them. Elisha then prayed that God would open the eyes of the young man to see the hosts of protective angels. "And the Lord opened the eyes of the young man; and he saw: and, behold, the mountain was full of horses and chariots of fire round about Elisha" (2 Kings 6:17).

The prophet Balaam couldn't see the angel standing in his path, though his donkey could, until "the Lord opened the eyes of Balaam, and he saw the angel of the Lord standing in the way, and his sword drawn in his hand" (Numbers 22:31).

They help in time of danger.

During a terrible storm on the Mediterranean that lasted for two weeks, Paul faced shipwreck with more than two hundred fifty other passengers. Though he was a prisoner on his way to Rome for trial, Paul encouraged his shipmates: "I urge you to keep up your courage, because not one of you will be lost; only the ship will be destroyed. Last night an angel of the God whose I am and whom I serve stood beside me and said, 'Do not be afraid, Paul. You must stand trial before Caesar; and God has graciously given you the lives of all who sail with you.' So keep up your courage, men, for I have faith in God that it will happen just as he told me. Nevertheless, we must run aground on some island" (Acts 27:22–25, NIV). Instead of being afraid, Paul chose to believe the angel's message that he and all the others would come out of the shipwreck all right.

There must be faith in God Who sends angels to help His people during times of hardship. Corrie ten Boom displayed this kind of faith when she entered Ravensbruck, the Nazi prison camp, during the time of Hitler's rage. She wrote the following:

Together we entered the terrifying building. At a table were women who took away all our possessions. Everyone had to undress completely and then go to a room where her hair was checked.

I asked a woman who was busy checking the possessions of the new arrivals if I might use the toilet. She pointed to a door, and I discovered that the convenience was nothing more than a hole in the shower-room floor. Betsie stayed close beside me all the time. Suddenly I had an inspiration. "Quick, take off your woolen underwear," I whispered to her. I rolled it up with mine and laid the bundle in a corner with my little Bible. The spot was alive with cockroaches, but I didn't worry about that. I felt wonderfully relieved and happy. "The Lord is busy answering our prayers, Betsie," I whispered. "We shall not have to make the sacrifice of all our clothes."

We hurried back to the row of women waiting to be undressed. A little later, after we had had our showers and put on our shirts and shabby dresses, I hid the roll of underwear and my Bible under my dress. It did bulge out obviously through my dress; but I prayed, "Lord, cause now thine angels to surround me; and let them not be transparent today, for the guards must not see me." I felt perfectly at ease. Calmly I passed the guards. Everyone was checked, from the front, the sides, the back. Not a bulge escaped the eyes of the guard. The woman just in front of me had hidden a woolen vest under her dress; it was taken from her. They let me pass, for they did not see me. Betsie, right behind me, was searched.

But outside awaited another danger. On each side of the door were women who looked everyone over for a second time. They felt over the body of each one who passed. I knew they would not see me, for the angels were still surrounding me. I was not even surprised when they passed me by; but within me rose the jubliant cry, "O Lord, if Thou dost so answer prayer, I can face even Ravensbruck unafraid."

Angels watch us and listen to our words.

"We are made a spectacle unto the world, and to angels, and to men," wrote the apostle Paul (1 Corinthians 4:9). Angels are interested spectators and watch all that we do.

The Book of Ecclesiastes (5:6) talks about vowing a vow and not keeping it. It signifies that angels hear what we say. "Suffer not thy mouth to cause thy flesh to sin; neither say thou before the angel, that it was an error: wherefore should God be angry at thy voice, and destroy the work of thine hands?"

Could it be that we tie the hands of the angels, who are around us, keeping them from working for us, because of the negative things that we confess? Although this verse is talking about making a vow to the Lord, it is quite evident that the angel God has assigned to us is listening to our voice.

There are warring angels who protect from harm, deliver from destruction—and destroy if the need arises.

• After Moses died, Joshua assumed the leadership over the children of Israel.

One day he was standing near the city of Jericho when he "looked up and saw a man standing in front of him a drawn sword in his hand. Joshua went up to him and asked, 'Are you for us or for our enemies?'

"'Neither,' he replied, 'but as commander of the army of the Lord I have now come'" (Joshua 5:13–14, NIV).

- Daniel speaks of the warfare that occurs sometimes when people pray. Daniel had been fasting and praying for twenty-one days when he had a vision of a shining angel that overwhelmed him. "A hand touched me and set me trembling on my hands and knees. He said, 'Daniel, you who are highly esteemed, consider carefully the words I am about to speak to you....' And when he said this to me, I stood up trembling.

  "Then he continued, 'Do not be afraid, Daniel. Since the first day that you set your mind to gain understanding and to humble yourself before your God, your words were heard, and I have come in response to them. But the prince of the Persian kingdom resisted me twenty-one days. Then Michael, one of the chief princes, came to help me, because I was detained there with the king of Persia'" (Daniel 10:4–14, NIV). Daniel was so overwhelmed by the angel's words, he nearly fainted. But the angel touched him and gave him strength.

- When the city of Jerusalem was surrounded by Assyrian forces and taunted by their king Sennacherib for believing that the Lord their God would save them, King Hezekiah and the prophet Isaiah prayed to God for help in this time of trouble. "And the Lord sent an angel, who annihilated all the fighting men and the leaders and officers in the camp of the Assyrian king. So he withdrew to his own land in disgrace. And when he went into the temple of his god, some of his sons cut him down with the sword.

  "So the Lord saved Hezekiah and the people of Jerusalem from the hand of Sennacherib king of Assyria and from the hand of all others. He took care of them on every side" (2 Chronicles 32:9–22, NIV).

2 Kings 19:35 (NIV) also gives an account of the power of this one warring angel. "That night the angel of the Lord went out and put to death a hundred and eighty-five thousand men in the Assyrian camp. When the people got up the next morning—there were all the dead bodies!"

- The prophet Balaam was summoned by Barak, king of Moab, to come and curse the Israelites who were invading the land. Though God told him the Israelites were blessed, Balaam saddled his donkey and went with the Moabite princes, anyway, against God's will. "God was very angry when he went, and the angel of the Lord stood in the road to oppose him.... When the donkey saw the angel of the Lord standing with a drawn sword in his hand, she turned off the road into a field. Balaam beat her, to get her back on the road" (Numbers 22:22–23, NIV). Balaam kept beating the donkey because she would not do what he wanted, but would stop in front of the angel. Finally God caused the donkey to talk. Even this amazing feat did not faze Balaam. Finally "the Lord opened Balaam's eyes, and he saw the angel of the Lord standing in the road with his sword drawn," barring the way. If the donkey hadn't moved aside, the angel told Balaam, "'I would certainly have killed you by now, but I would spare her'" (Numbers 22:31–33, NIV).

- When David prayed for safety from his enemies, he asked the Lord to "let them be as chaff before the wind: and let the angel of the Lord chase them. Let their way be dark and slippery: and let the angel of the Lord persecute them" (Psalm 35:5–6). David knew about the warring angels because when he had sinned in numbering the people, God had let him see the angel that was destroying the people with a pestilence. "And when the angel stretched out his hand upon Jerusalem to destroy it, the Lord repented him of the evil, and said to the angel that destroyed the people, It is enough: stay now thine hand. And the angel of the Lord was by the threshingplace of Araunah the Jebusite. And David spake unto the Lord when he saw the angel that smote the people, and said, Lo I have sinned" (2 Samuel 24:16–17).

- When Herod (Agrippa) delivered an address before a crowd of his subjects, the people shouted out, "It is the voice of a god, and not of a man. And immediately the angel of the Lord smote him, because he gave not God the glory: and he was eaten of worms, and gave up the ghost" (Acts 12:22–23).

- Jesus told us: "The Son of man shall send forth his angels, and they shall gather out of his kingdom all things that offend, and them which do iniquity; And shall cast them into a furnace of fire: there shall be wailing and gnashing of teeth. Then shall the righteous shine forth as the sun in the kingdom of their Father" (Matthew 13:41–43).

- Jesus also said: "So shall it be at the end of the world: the angels shall come forth, and sever the wicked from among the just. And shall cast them into the furnace of fire: there shall be wailing and gnashing of teeth" (Matthew 13:49–50).

All of God's children have angels.

- "The angel of the Lord encampeth round about them that fear him, and delivereth them." (Psalm 34:7).

- When the disciples argued about who was greatest in God's kingdom, Jesus called a little child into the group and told them they had to become like children, that those who would humble themselves as the child would be great. If anyone offended the child he said, the offender was in great trouble. "'See that you do not look down on one of these little ones. For I tell you that their angels in heaven always see the face of my Father in heaven'" (Matthew 18:10, NIV).

- When Abraham learned that God was getting ready to destroy Sodom and Gomorrah, he was so concerned about his nephew Lot and his family in Sodom that he interceded with God to save the city from destruction, but there were not enough righteous people in the city to save it. Because of God's great respect for Abraham, however, he sent two angels to rescue Lot. On the day the city was to be destroyed, the angels had to force Lot and his wife to hurry and get out. "With the coming of dawn, the angels urged Lot, saying, 'Hurry! Take your wife, and your two daughters who are here, or you will be swept away when the city is punished.'

  "When he hesitated, the men [angels] grasped his hand and the hands of his wife and of his two daughters, and led them safely out of the city, for the Lord was merciful to them" (Genesis 19:15–16, NIV).

- In Jesus' parable of the rich man and Lazarus, he pictures Lazarus, the beggar, as having an angelic escort after his death. "And it came to pass, that the beggar died, and was carried by the angels into Abraham's bosom" (Luke 16:22).

- Psalm 91:11 says, "For he shall give his angels charge over thee, to keep thee in all thy ways."

There are ministering angels.

- After his baptism, Jesus went on a forty-day fast. At the end of it, the devil came to tempt him. Jesus refused the temptations through quoting God's Word. Then the devil left him, "and, behold, angels came and ministered unto him" (Matthew 4:11).

- An angel also ministered to Jesus in the garden of Gethsemane, giving him strength for the coming ordeal (Luke 22:42).

- After his victory over the idolatrous prophets. Elijah had to flee from Queen Jezebel's threats. In the desert, he gave up, and wanted to die. "And as he lay and slept under a juniper tree, behold, then an angel touched him, and said unto him, Arise and eat. And he looked, and, behold, there was a cake baken on the coals, and a cruse of water at his head. And he did eat and drink, and laid him down again. And the angel of the Lord came again the second time and touched him, and said, Arise and eat; because the journey is too great for thee" (1 Kings 19:5–7).

Angels receive their instructions from God and are under his authority.

- When David sinned by numbering the people, God gave him a choice of punishment. David chose to fall into the hands of God because God was more merciful than man. Because of David's sin, God sent a pestilence upon Israel and seventy thousand men died. I Chronicles 21:15 shows the authority of God over the angels. "God sent an angel unto Jerusalem to destroy it; and as he was destroying, the Lord beheld, and he repented him of the evil, and said to the angel that destroyed, It is enough, stay now thine hand. And the angel of the Lord stood by the threshingfloor of Ornan the Jebusite." At the angel's direction, David erected an altar at that place, which later became the site of Solomon's temple (2 Chronicles 21:18–30; 22:1).

- Psalm 103:20 says, "Bless the Lord, ye his angels that excel in strength, that do his commandments, hearkening unto the voice of his word."

God promised to send an angel before his people.

- When Abraham told his servant to go back to Haran and find a wife for his son Isaac among his relatives, he told the servant that "the Lord shall send his angel before thee" (Genesis 24:7). The servant testified that his journey was successful because the Lord had indeed sent his angel ahead to prepare the way (Genesis 24:40, 48).

- When the Israelites were caught between the Red Sea and the oncoming Egyptian army, "the angel of God, who had been traveling in front of Israel's army, withdrew and stood behind them. The pillar of cloud also moved from in front and stood behind them, coming between the army of Egypt and Israel. Throughout the night the cloud brought darkness to the one side and light to the other side; so neither went near the other all night long" (Exodus 14:19–20, NIV). As a result the Israelites were free to cross the Red Sea.

- At Mt. Sinai, God gave the Ten Commandments and then promised the children of Israel, "'See, I am sending the angel ahead of you to guard you along the way and to bring you to the place I have prepared. Pay attention to him and listen to what he says. Do not rebel against him; he will not forgive your rebellion, since my Name is in him. If you listen carefully to what he says and do all that I say, I will be an enemy to your enemies and will oppose those who oppose you. My angel will go ahead of you'" (Exodus 23:20–22, NIV).

- Later, even after the Israelites sinned by making a golden calf and worshiping it, God still promised to lead them. Sinners would be punished, God said to Moses, but the journey would go on. "'Whoever has sinned again me I will blot out of my book. Now go, lead the people to the place I spoke of, and my angel will go before you'" (Numbers 32:33–34, NIV).

- God repeated the promise to Moses as the people got ready to move. "'Leave this place, you and the people you brought up out of Egypt....I will send an angel before you'" (Numbers 33:1–2, NIV).

The Bible records many encounters with angels.

The following individuals met or saw angelic beings. Where we have already dicussed their encounters, I will refer you to those page numbers.

Abraham

See page 126.

Abraham was asked by God to offer Isaac, his son, as a burnt-offering. Abraham took Isaac and they took a three-day journey together to a mountain, where they climbed to the top and built an altar. Just as Abraham pulled the knife back to thrust it into the heart of his son, "the angel of the Lord called unto him out of heaven, and said, Abraham, Abraham: and he said, Here am I." The call came to save him from doing what he did not want to do, and showed him a ram for the sacrifice. (Genesis 22:11) "And the angel of the Lord called unto Abraham out of heaven the second time....By myself have I sworn, saith the Lord...that in blessing I will bless thee" (v. 15).

Hagar

- Hagar had two angelic encounters. The first one occurred after she fled from the abuse of Sarah, her mistress. She had been given to Abram so she could bear him children, since Sarah could not bear children. When Sarah saw that the pregnant Hagar was becoming arrogant and despising her, Sarah began to mistreat her.

   Hagar ran away into the desert, "and the angel of the Lord found her by a fountain of water in the wilderness" (Genesis 16:7). The angel told her to return to her mistress and submit to her, for the child she would bear would be called Ishmael and he would become a loner, living in opposition to other people. Hagar obeyed the angel of the Lord and went back.

- Thirteen years later, after Sarah had borne a son Isaac, she saw Ishmael taunting Isaac. She told Abraham that the camp was not big enough for two wives and two sons, and that Hagar had to leave. So Abraham sent Hagar and Ishmael away, with a few provisions, into the wilderness of Beersheba. When their water was gone, Hagar sat down and wept for her thirsty son. "The angel of God called to Hagar from heaven and said to her, 'What is the matter, Hagar? Do not be afraid.'" He told her God would make her son a great nation. "Then God opened her eyes and she saw a well of water. So she went and filled the skin with water and gave the boy a drink" (Genesis 21:17–19, NIV).

Jacob

- Jacob had a dream in which he saw a great ladder reaching from earth to heaven, and the angels of God were ascending and descending on it. There above it stood the Lord, and he said: "I am the Lord, the God of your father Abraham and the God of Isaac....I am with you and will watch over you wherever you go, and I will bring you back to this land. I will not leave you until I have done what I have promised you" (Genesis 28:13–15, NIV). When Jacob woke up, his reaction was one of fear, "Surely the Lord is in this place!" (v. 16).

- Years later, when Jacob was returning to Canaan with a large family, and was fearful of his meeting with his brother Esau, "the angels of God met him. And when Jacob saw them, he said, 'This is God's host'" (Genesis 32:1–2).

Balaam

See pages 120, 124.

Joshua

See pages 122–23.

Gideon

In the time of the judges, an angel of the Lord appeared to Gideon, who was hiding from the Midianites and their marauding bands, and told him, "The Lord is with you, mighty warrior." When the Lord told Gideon he was to be the leader of the Israelites against the Midianites, Gideon first had excuses and then asked for a sign that this messenger was really from God. He would bring an offering and asked the angel to wait for him. After he'd cooked a goat, he brought it out with its broth and some unleavened bread. The angel directed him to put the food on a rock and to pour out the broth. When he did so, "with the tip of the staff that was in his hand, the angel of the Lord touched the meat and the unleavened bread. Fire flared from the rock, consuming the meat and the bread. And the angel of the Lord disappeared. When Gideon realized that it was the angel of the Lord, he exclaimed, 'Ah, Sovereign Lord! I have seen the angel of the Lord face to face!'

"But the Lord said to him, 'Peace! Do not be afraid. You are not going to die'" (Judges 6:20–22, NIV).

Manoah's wife *(Samson's mother)*

Manoah and his wife had never been able to have children. One day "the angel of the Lord appeared to her and said, 'You are sterile and childless, but you are going to conceive and have a son'" (Judges 13:3, NIV). He gave her instructions on how to raise him so he would be devoted to the Lord. She rushed to report to her husband that a man of God who looked like an awesome angel of God had come to her (v. 6). Manoah wanted to hear the news and get the directions for himself, and he prayed that God would send the man of God back to them.

"God heard Manoah, and the angel of God came again to the woman while she was out in the field; but her husband Manoah was not with her. The woman hurried to tell her husband, 'He's here! the man who appeared to me the other day!'" (vv. 9–10, NIV). The angel gave Manoah the same instructions his wife had received. Then Manoah asked the angel to eat with them, still unaware that he was an angel. The angel said he would not eat, but that they could afford a burnt offering to the Lord. Manoah wanted to know the angel's name, so they could honor him when his prophecy came true. That was a secret, the angel told them, "beyond understanding" (v. 18, NIV). So Manoah offered a kid as a burnt offering. "And the Lord did an amazing thing while Manoah and his wife watched: As the flame blazed up from the altar toward heaven, the angel of the Lord ascended in the flame. Seeing this, Manoah and his wife fell with their faces to the ground. When the angel of the Lord did not show himself again to Manoah and his wife, Manoah realized that it was the angel of the Lord....

"The woman gave birth to a boy and named him Samson" (vv. 18–21, 24, NIV).

David

See page 127.

Elijah

See page 127.

Elisha

See page 120.

Ezekiel

Ezekiel had many visions of angels and especially of the cherubim with their wheels within wheels and four-sided bodies. For his description of the cherubim, read Ezekiel 1 and 10.

Shadrach, Meshach and Abednego

When King Nebuchadnezzar had the three Hebrew young men thrown in to the fiery furnace, something miraculous happened. The king described it like this: "Praise be to the God of Shadrach, Meshach and Abednego, who has sent his angel and rescued his servants! They trust in him and defied the king's command and were willing to give up their lives rather than serve or worship any god except their own God" (Daniel 3:28, NIV). The three young men came out of the furnace with not one hair singed, no burns on their bodies, no smell of fire on them or their clothes. It was a miracle!

Daniel

Daniel was thrown into the lion's den because of evil plans made by jealous courtiers of King Darius. Daniel prayed and God sent an angel to protect him. Unaware of this, King Darius was unable to sleep all night. When the dawn came, the king hurried to the den and "called to Daniel in an anguished voice, 'Daniel, servant of the living God, has your God, whom you serve continually, been able to rescue you from the lions?'

"'Daniel answered, 'O king, live forever! My God sent his angel, and he shut the mouths of the lions. They have not hurt me'" (Daniel 6:20–22, NIV).

See also page 88.

Zechariah, the prophet

Zechariah had eight visions in which an angel of the Lord taught him through pictures and symbols how the little group of returned exiles was to live in obedience to God. (See Zechariah 1:7–6:8.) One of the visions (4:1–14) was of a seven-branched lampstand fed constant olive oil from two olive trees on each side. The angel told Zechariah that the nation and leaders of Israel—the lampstand—could only be strong and keep going by God's power—the oil. "'Not by might nor by power, but by my Spirit,' says the Lord Almighty" (4:6, NIV).

Zechariah, the priest

Zechariah (Zacharias in KJV), a priest, was burning incense in the temple of the Lord in Jerusalem, when "an angel appeared to him, standing on the right side of the altar of incense. When Zechariah saw him, he was startled and was gripped with fear. But the angel said to him, 'Do not be afraid, Zechariah; your prayer has been heard. Your wife Elizabeth will bear you a son, and you are to give him the name John'" (Luke 1:11–13, NIV).

Zechariah asked the angel how this could be, since he was an old man and his wife was also old. "The angel answered, 'I am Gabriel. I stand in the presence of God, and I have been sent to speak to you and to tell you this good news'" (Luke 1:19, NIV).

Mary

Six months after that appearance, "God sent the angel Gabriel to Nazareth, a town in Galilee, to a virgin pledged to be married to a man named Joseph...
[whose] name was Mary....the angel said to her, 'Do not be afraid, Mary; you have found favor with God. You will be with child and give birth to a son and

you are to give him the name Jesus....The Holy Spirit will come upon you, and the power of the Most High will overshadow you'" (Luke 1:26–27, 30–32, 35, NIV).

Joseph

- When Joseph thought to hide his fiancée Mary from the public eye because she was pregnant before their marriage, Matthew 1:20 (NIV) says that "after he had considered this, an angel of the Lord appeared to him in a dream and said, 'Joseph, son of David, do not be afraid to take Mary home as your wife, because what is conceived in her is from the Holy Spirit.'" Joseph obeyed the angel's word.

- Some time after Jesus was born, an angel appeared to Joseph again in a dream and told him to hurry "and take the child and his mother and escape into Egypt. Stay there until I tell you, for Herod is going to search for the child to kill him" (Matthew 2:13, NIV). Again Joseph obeyed, and Jesus' life was spared.

- A third angel visitation in a dream came to Joseph in Egypt, telling him it was safe now to return to Israel, because Herod was dead (Matthew 2:19–20).

The Shepherds

When Jesus was born in Bethlehem, an angel appeared to shepherds in the fields near the town, and the glory of the Lord shone around them. As the angel announced the birth of the Savior, the Christ, "suddenly there was with the angel a multitude of the heavenly host praising God, and saying, Glory to God in the highest, and on earth peace, good will toward men" (Luke 2:23–24).

Jesus

See pages 126–27.

Mary Magdalene and the other women

"After the sabbath, at dawn on the first day of the week, Mary Magdalene and the other Mary went to look at the tomb.

"There was a violent earthquake, for an angel of the Lord came down from heaven and, going to the tomb, rolled back the stone and sat on it. His appearance was like lightning, and his clothes were white as snow....

"And the angel said to the women, 'Do not be afraid, for I know that you are looking for Jesus, who was crucified. He is not here; he has risen, just as he said....go quickly and tell his disciples: "He has risen from the dead"'" (Matthew 28:1–7, NIV).

See also Mark 16:1–7; Luke 24:1–8.

The Apostles

There came a great healing revival to the young church in Jerusalem after the sudden death of Ananias and Sapphira, the husband and wife who lied to the Holy Spirit. The church and the apostles were looked upon with both fear and respect, and the church grew in numbers. The whole scenario filled the high priest and the Sadducees with indignation and jealousy. "They arrested the apostles and put them in the public jail. But during the night an angel of the Lord opened the doors of the jail, and brought them out. 'Go, stand in the temple courts,' he said, 'and tell the people the full message of this new life'" (Acts 5:18–20, NIV).

Cornelius

Cornelius was a centurion in the Roman army in Caesarea, who believed in God. One day he had a vision. In the vision an angel appeared and told him to send messengers south to Joppa and ask for Peter. The next day in Joppa, Peter was on the roof of his house praying. He became hungry, and God sent him a vision in which he was told to eat food the Jews considered unclean. God told him not to call impure what God had made clean. Just then the messengers from Cornelius knocked on the door. God told Peter he was to go with them into a Gentile house— something as a Jew he was forbidden to do and which made him very uncomfortable. But because of Cornelius's vision and his vision, he went, to give the good news of Jesus Christ to a non-Jew, a Roman. So the door of the gospel was opened to the Gentiles by the miraculous intervention of God through an angel and visions sent to key people. God's plan was accomplished. The account is given in Acts 10.

Philip

Philip was one of the Greek-speaking men elected to serve in the church at Jerusalem (Acts 6:5). He had been holding a successful mission in Samaria when "an angel of the Lord said to Philip, 'Go south to the road—the desert road— that goes down from Jerusalem to Gaza'" (Acts 8:28, NIV). On that road he came up to an Ethiopian eunuch, an important treasury official in the Ethiopian court, sitting in his chariot, reading aloud from Isaiah 53—but without understanding it. Philip was able to tell him "the good news about Jesus," and to baptize him as a new Christian (Acts 8:26–39).

Peter

Some time after the angel freed the apostles from the prison in Jerusalem, James was arrested by Herod, and executed, pleasing the enemies of the Christians. So

Herod arrested Peter and planned to execute him after the Passover. The church prayed hard for him. The night before his trial was to begin, Peter was asleep in his cell, chained to two guards. "Suddenly an angel of the Lord appeared and a light shone in the cell. He struck Peter on the side and woke him up. 'Quick, get up!' he said, and the chains fell off Peter's wrists.

"Then the angel said to him, 'Put on your clothes and sandals.' And Peter did so. 'Wrap your cloak around you and follow me,' the angel told him. Peter followed him out of the prison, but he had no idea that what the angel was doing was really happening; he thought he was seeing a vision. They passed the first and second guards and came to the iron gate leading to the city. It opened for them by itself, and they went through it. When they had walked the length of one street, suddenly the angel left him.

"Then Peter came to himself and said, 'Now I know without a doubt that the Lord sent his angel and rescued me from Herod's clutches'" (Acts 12:6–11 NIV).

Paul

The Apostle Paul had several encounters with the heavenly world of the spirit and miracles. First of all, he was knocked down on the road to Damascus by a bright light from heaven which blinded him for several days. He was headed to Damascus to arrest and imprison those who believed in Jesus as the Christ. A voice said to him, "Saul, Saul, why do you persecute me?"

"'Who are you, Lord?' Saul asked.

"'I am Jesus, whom you are persecuting,' he replied. 'Now get up and go into the city, and you will be told what you must do.'

"The men traveling with Saul stood there speechless; they heard the sound but did not see anyone" (Acts 9:3–7, NIV).

In Philippi, Paul and Silas were beaten and imprisoned for preaching about the

One Paul had encountered on the road to Damascus. While they were in prison, they sang praises to God. "About midnight ... suddenly there was such a violent earthquake that the foundations of the prison were shaken. At once all the prison doors flew open, and everybody's chains came loose" (Acts 16:25–26, NIV).

In Corinth, after Paul experienced persecution, "the Lord spoke to Paul in a vision: 'Do not be afraid; keep on speaking, do not be silent. For I am with you, and no one is going to attack and harm you, because I have many people in this city'" (Acts 18:9–10, NIV).

In Jerusalem, after a riot in the Sanhedrin where Paul was in danger of being physically attacked, "the following night the Lord stood near Paul and said, 'Take courage! As you have testified about me in Jerusalem, so you must also testify in Rome'" (Acts 23:11, NIV).

For the visit of an angel on board ship, see pages 120–21.

John

John, the author of the Book of Revelation, records his sweeping visions of heaven and the angelic hosts. Rather than list every one of his references to angels, I will just mention a few.

- The tens of thousands of angels in heaven continually praise God (5:11–12; 7:11–12; 19:1–8).

- John saw four angels standing at the four corners of the earth holding the four winds (7:1).

- The angels are involved in judgment, which John saw and heard as trumpet blasts (8 and 9), and as bowls of disasters poured out on the earth (15 and 16).

- Angels announced the future to John (14:6–12; 22:6), and also directed him to write down what he was seeing (14:13; 19:9). Once the angel told John not to write what he was hearing (10:1—4).

- Angels explained to John what he was seeing, sometimes to him personally, and sometimes to the whole world (17 and 18).

- John saw an angel who had the power to lock Satan up for a thousand years (20:1—4).

They had faces that were all of living flame,
And wings of gold, and all the rest so white,
There is no snow that could compare with it.
When, tier by tier, they sank into the flower,
They made offerings of the peace and ardor
That they garnered from the fanning of their wings.

—DANTE ALIGHIERI (1265–1321)
Paradiso, XXXI

~ *Reader's Response* ~

IF YOU HAVE AN ANGEL STORY, or have had a supernatural experience, or an encounter with the invisible world, and would like to contribute your story to the next book on angels, please send your story to the following address:

Joy Haney
7149 E. 8 Mile Road
Stockton, CA 95212
U.S.A.

~

A NOTE FROM THE EDITORS

This book was selected by the book division of the company that publishes *Guideposts*, a monthly magazine filled with true stories of people's adventures in faith, and *Angels on Earth*, a bimonthly magazine that presents true stories about God's angels and humans who have played angelic roles in daily life.

Guideposts magazine and *Angels on Earth* are not sold on the newsstand. They are available by subscription only. And subscribing is easy. All you have to do is write to Guideposts, 39 Seminary Hill Road, Carmel, New York 10512.

When you subscribe, you can count on receiving exciting new evidence of God's presence, His guidance and His limitless love for all of us.

Guideposts is also available on the Internet by accessing our homepage on the World Wide Web at http://www.guideposts.org. Send prayer requests to our Monday morning Prayer Fellowship. Read stories from recent issues of our magazines, *Guideposts*, *Angels on Earth*, *Guideposts for Kids* and *Positive Living*, and follow our popular book of daily devotionals, *Daily Guideposts*. Excerpts from some of our best-selling books are also available.